Experiencing
Choral Music

INTERMEDIATE

MIXED

Developed by

HAL•LEONARD® CORPORATION

Mc Graw Hill **Glencoe**

New York, New York   Columbus, Ohio   Chicago, Illinois   Peoria, Illinois   Woodland Hills, California

The portions of the National Standards for Music Education included here are reprinted from **National Standards for Arts Education** with permission from MENC–The National Association for Music Education. All rights reserved. Copyright © 1994 by MENC. The complete National Standards and additional materials relating to the Standards are available from MENC, 1806 Robert Fulton Drive, Reston, VA 20191 (telephone 800-336-3768).

A portion of the sales of this material goes to support music education programs through programs of MENC–The National Association for Music Education.

 **Glencoe**

*The **McGraw·Hill** Companies*

Printed in the United States of America.

Send all inquiries to:
Glencoe/McGraw-Hill
21600 Oxnard Street, Suite 500
Woodland Hills, CA 91367

ISBN 0-07-861108-3 (Student Edition)
ISBN 0-07-861109-1 (Teacher Wraparound Edition)

7 8 9 10 11 12   045   12 11 10 09 08 07

Credits

LEAD AUTHORS

Emily Crocker
Vice President of Choral Publications
Hal Leonard Corporation, Milwaukee, Wisconsin
Founder and Artistic Director, Milwaukee Children's Choir

Michael Jothen
Professor of Music, Program Director of Graduate Music Education
Chairperson of Music Education
Towson University, Towson, Maryland

Jan Juneau
Choral Director
Klein Collins High School
Spring, Texas

Henry H. Leck
Associate Professor and Director of Choral Activities
Butler University, Indianapolis, Indiana
Founder and Artistic Director, Indianapolis Children's Choir

Michael O'Hern
Choral Director
Lake Highlands High School
Richardson, Texas

Audrey Snyder
Composer
Eugene, Oregon

Mollie Tower
Coordinator of Choral and General Music, K-12, Retired
Austin, Texas

AUTHORS

Anne Denbow
Voice Instructor, Professional Singer/Actress
Director of Music, Holy Cross Episcopal Church
Simpsonville, South Carolina

Rollo A. Dilworth
Director of Choral Activities and Music
  Education
North Park University, Chicago, Illinois

Deidre Douglas
Choral Director
Aragon Middle School, Houston, Texas

Ruth E. Dwyer
Associate Director and Director of Education
Indianapolis Children's Choir
Indianapolis, Indiana

Norma Freeman
Choral Director
Saline High School, Saline, Michigan

Cynthia I. Gonzales
Music Theorist
Greenville, South Carolina

Michael Mendoza
Professor of Choral Activities
New Jersey State University
Trenton, New Jersey

Thomas Parente
Associate Professor
Westminster Choir College of Rider University
Princeton, New Jersey

Barry Talley
Director of Fine Arts and Choral Director
Deer Park ISD, Deer Park, Texas

CONTRIBUTING AUTHORS

Debbie Daniel
Choral Director, Webb Middle School
Garland, Texas

Roger Emerson
Composer/Arranger
Mount Shasta, California

Kari Gilbertson
Choral Director, Forest Meadow Junior High
Richardson, Texas

Tim McDonald
Creative Director, Music Theatre International
New York, New York

Christopher W. Peterson
Assistant Professor of Music Education (Choral)
University of Wisconsin-Milwaukee
Milwaukee, Wisconsin

Kirby Shaw
Composer/Arranger
Ashland, Oregon

Stephen Zegree
Professor of Music
Western Michigan State University
Kalamazoo, Michigan

EDITORIAL

Linda Rann
Senior Editor
Hal Leonard Corporation
Milwaukee, Wisconsin

Stacey Nordmeyer
Choral Editor
Hal Leonard Corporation
Milwaukee, Wisconsin

Table of Contents

Introductory Materials . . . . i-viii

Lessons

1 **Rise Up This Day To Celebrate • 3-Part Mixed** 2
   Michael Haydn, arranged by Patrick Liebergen

2 **Down In The Valley • 3-Part Mixed** 10
   American Folk Song, arranged by Linda Spevacek

3 **Elijah Rock! • 3-Part Mixed** 16
   Traditional Spiritual, arranged by Roger Emerson

   Spotlight On Diction 25

4 **America The Beautiful • 3-Part Mixed** 26
   Samuel A. Ward, arranged by Joyce Eilers Bacak

   Spotlight On Posture 35

5 **Cantemos Alleluia • SAB** 36
   Emily Crocker

6 **Winter Storm • 3-Part Mixed** 46
   Audrey Snyder

   Spotlight On Vowels 55

7 **Shalom Aleichem • SAB** 56
   I. and S. E. Goldfarb, arranged by Gil Aldema
   edited by J. Mark Dunn

   Spotlight On Arranging 63

8 **Calypso Gloria • SATB** 64
   Emily Crocker

   Spotlight On Pitch Matching 77

9 **Innsbruck, ich muss dich lassen • SATB** 78
   Heinrich Isaac, arranged by John Leavitt

Spotlight On Breath Management 83

10 **Come Joyfully Sing • SAB** 84
George Frideric Handel, arranged by Patrick M. Liebergen

11 **Bless The Lord, O My Soul • 3-Part Mixed** 92
Mikhail Ippolitov-Ivanov, arranged by Joyce Eilers

Spotlight On Concert Etiquette 99

12 **Sing To The Lord from *Three Meditations* • SATB** 100
Noel Goemanne

Music & History

Renaissance Period 108

Baroque Period 112

Classical Period 116

Romantic Period 120

Contemporary Period 124

Spotlight On Careers In Music 128

Choral Library

¡Aleluya, Amén! • SATB 130
Rafael D. Grullón

Spotlight On Changing Voice 135

Bound For The Rio Grande • 3-Part Mixed 136
American Sea Chantey, arranged by Emily Crocker

Spotlight On Gospel Music 147

City Called Heaven • SATB 148
Traditional Spiritual, arranged by Josephine Poelinitz

Duond Akuru • SAB 156
Rollo A. Dilworth

I Know Where I'm Goin' • 2-Part Mixed 168
Irish Folk Song, arranged by Chris Moore

Spotlight On Improvisation 177

Kyrie • SAB 178
Andrea Klouse

Lakota Wiyanki • SATB 186
Judith Herrington and Gail Woodside

Miserere Nobis • 3-Part Mixed 194
Victor Johnson

Spotlight On Musical Theater 203

The River Sleeps Beneath The Sky • 3-Part Mixed 204
Mary Lynn Lightfoot

Set Me As A Seal • SATB 212
John Leavitt

Sing Out This Maytime • SAB 216
Johann Hermann Schein, arranged by Patrick Liebergen

The Wells Fargo Wagon • SAB 227
Meredith Willson, arranged by Roger Emerson

Glossary 239

Classified Index 253

Index of Songs and Spotlights 255

TO THE STUDENT

Welcome to choir!

By singing in the choir, you have chosen to be a part of an exciting and rewarding adventure. The benefits of being in choir are many. Basically, singing is fun. It provides an expressive way of sharing your feelings and emotions. Through choir, you will have friends that share a common interest with you. You will experience the joy of making beautiful music together. Choir provides the opportunity to develop your interpersonal skills. It takes teamwork and cooperation to sing together, and you must learn how to work with others. As you critique your individual and group performances, you can improve your ability to analyze and communicate your thoughts clearly.

Even if you do not pursue a music career, music can be an important part of your life. There are many avocational opportunities in music. **Avocational** means *not related to a job or career*. Singing as a hobby can provide you with personal enjoyment, enrich your life, and teach you life skills. Singing is something you can do for the rest of your life.

In this course, you will be presented with the basic skills of vocal production and music literacy. You will be exposed to songs from different cultures, songs in many different styles and languages, and songs from various historical periods. You will discover connections between music and the other arts. Guidelines for becoming a better singer and choir member include:

- Come to class prepared to learn.
- Respect the efforts of others.
- Work daily to improve your sight-singing skills.
- Sing expressively at all times.
- Have fun singing.

This book was written to provide you with a meaningful choral experience. Take advantage of the knowledge and opportunities offered here. Your exciting adventure of experiencing choral music is about to begin!

Lessons

Lessons for the Beginning of the Year

1 Rise Up This Day To Celebrate 2

2 Down In The Valley 10

3 Elijah Rock! 16

4 America The Beautiful 26

Lessons for Mid-Winter

5 Cantemos Alleluia 36

6 Winter Storm .46

7 Shalom Aleichem 56

8 Calypso Gloria 64

Lessons for Concert/Festival

9   Innsbruck, ich muss dich lassen 78

10 Come Joyfully Sing 84

11 Bless The Lord, O My Soul 92

12 Sing To The Lord 100

Rise Up This Day To Celebrate

Composer: Johann Michael Haydn (1737–1806), arranged by Patrick M. Liebergen
Text: English Text by Patrick M. Liebergen
Voicing: 3-Part Mixed

VOCABULARY

Classical period

mass

phrase

cadence

trio

Focus

• Describe and perform music from the Classical period.

• Sing phrases using repetition and contrast.

• Identify and perform cadences.

Getting Started

Have you ever noticed that great talent sometimes runs in families?

Venus & Serena Williams	*Professional tennis players*
Donny & Marie Osmond	*Professional singers*
Charlotte & Emily Bronte	*English novelists*
Wilhelm & C. P. E. Bach	*Composers (sons of J.S. Bach)*

The talent and skills of the famous siblings mentioned above are extraordinary. The same could also be said of the Haydn brothers. Although we remember Franz Joseph (1732–1809) for his "Surprise Symphony," his younger brother Johann Michael was a prolific composer, as well.

To learn more about the Classical period, see page 116.

◆ History and Culture

Johann Michael Haydn (1737–1806) was a well-known Austrian composer during the **Classical period** *(1750–1820)*. Like the best male singers of his time, he left home at the age of eight or nine to attend St. Stephen's Cathedral school in Vienna. As an adult, he held the important position of court musician and composer for the Archbishop of Salzburg.

Among his compositions, Haydn wrote 38 masses for choir and orchestra. A **mass** is *a religious service of prayers and ceremonies consisting of spoken and sung sections.* This arrangement of "Rise Up This Day To Celebrate" is from his *Deutsche Messe* of 1777.

Links to Learning

◆ Vocal

Music of the Classical period sometimes features repetition with contrasts. One such contrast is to repeat a **phrase**, or *a musical idea with a beginning and an end*, using a change in dynamics. In "Rise Up This Day To Celebrate," each phrase is repeated at a softer dynamic level. Perform the following phrase twice, first time *forte* (loud) and second time *piano* (soft), to practice these contrasts.

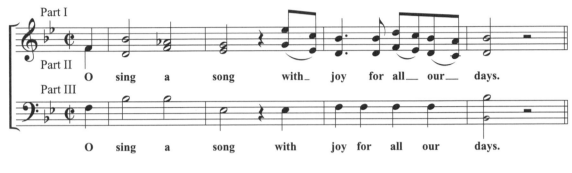

◆ Theory

Just as a period indicates the end of a sentence, a **cadence** is *a melodic or harmonic structure that marks the end of a phrase or the completion of a song.* The first cadence in "Rise Up This Day To Celebrate" appears in measures 7–8. Perform the following example on "loo" to practice singing this cadence.

Evaluation

Demonstrate how well you have learned the skills and concepts featured in the lesson "Rise Up This Day To Celebrate" by completing the following:

• Discuss the musical characteristics of the Classical period.

• As a **trio** (*three singers*) with one singer on a part, perform measures 17–28 with accuracy, showing your understanding of dynamic contrast in each phrase. How well did you show dynamic contrast?

• With two or three classmates, analyze the music and locate the cadences similar to the example found in the Theory section above. Share your findings. In what ways do the cadences provide organization and structure to this piece?

Rise Up This Day To Celebrate

For 3-Part Mixed and Piano with Optional B♭ Trumpet*

Arranged with English Text by
PATRICK M. LIEBERGEN

JOHANN MICHAEL HAYDN
(1737–1806)

*Part for B♭ Trumpet may be found on page 9.

cheer - ful sound— we— raise.

cheer - ful sound we raise.

poco rit.
poco rit.
poco rit.
poco rit.

Rise

31
a tempo
a tempo

up this day to cel - e - brate! Come cel - e - brate! Re -

a tempo

31

a tempo

joice! Rise up this day to cel - e - brate! Now

wel - come— ev - 'ry voice! Rise up, sing a

song to - day!— Re - joice!

Rise Up This Day To Celebrate

Bb TRUMPET

JOHANN MICHAEL HAYDN (1737–1806)
Arranged with English Text by PATRICK M. LIEBERGEN

Down In The Valley

Composer: American Folk Song, arranged by Linda Spevacek
Text: Traditional
Voicing: 3-Part Mixed

VOCABULARY

lyrics

folk song

intonation

breath support

$\frac{3}{4}$ meter

 SKILL BUILDERS

To learn more about
$\frac{3}{4}$ *meter, see*
Intermediate Sight-
Singing, *page 17.*

Focus

- Read and perform music in $\frac{3}{4}$ meter.

- Define and demonstrate accurate intonation.

- Read, write and perform music in the key of E♭ major.

Getting Started

Roses love sunshine, violets love dew
Angels in heaven know I love you.

What is the theme or subject matter of this short poem? If you guessed "love," then you are correct. More songs have been written about love than any other subject. Some people find it easier to express their feelings and emotions through music then through the spoken word. "Down In The Valley" is a beautiful song that expresses love through the words and music. Look at the **lyrics** *(the words to a song),* and find other passages that express one's love in a unique way.

◆ History and Culture

"Down In The Valley" is an American folk song. **Folk songs** are *songs that have been passed down by word of mouth from generation to generation.* They sometimes reflect a local place or event, and they were often the popular songs of the day. Although the exact origin of "Down In The Valley" is unknown, it is believed to be from the Kentucky area. Many versions of this song exist.

The lyrics of "Down In The Valley" read like a poem. Many song texts are taken from poetry. Create your own lyrics by writing an original poem in the style and format of the verses of this song. The last word of each line should rhyme. Share your new lyrics with the class.

Links to Learning

◆ **Vocal**

Good **intonation,** or *in-tune singing,* is the product of proper breath support and vowel shape. **Breath support** refers to *the constant airflow necessary to produce sound for singing.* You can help develop this skill by doing the following:

> Breathe in air through an imaginary straw. Exhale on a hissing sound. First inhale on 4 counts, and then exhale over 6 counts, then 10 counts, then 12.

"Down in the Valley" is in the key of E♭ major and is based on the E♭ major scale. This scale uses the notes E♭, F, G, A♭, B♭, C, D, E♭. Sing the following E♭ major scale.

| E♭ | F | G | A♭ | B♭ | C | D | E♭ | D | C | B♭ | A♭ | G | F | E♭ |
| do | re | mi | fa | sol | la | ti | do | ti | la | sol | fa | mi | re | do |

◆ **Theory**

¾ **meter** is *a meter in which there are three beats per measure and the quarter note receives the beat.* Read and perform the following example to practice reading rhythmic patterns in ¾ meter.

ti ti ti ti ti ti   ta–a   ta   ta ta ta   tam   ti ta   ta–a–a–a–a–a

Evaluation

Demonstrate how well you have learned the skills and concepts featured in the lesson "Down In The Valley" by completing the following:

- Sing your part in measures 9–20 to show your understanding of ¾ meter and accurate intonation. How did you do?

- Using the pitches *do, re, mi, sol* and *la,* of the E♭ major scale, compose a melody in ¾ meter that begins and ends on *do.* Use rhythms found in "Down In The Valley." Notate your melody on staff paper or computer. With a classmate, check your work for correct rhythm and pitch notation.

Down In The Valley

For 3-Part Mixed, a cappella

**Arranged by
LINDA SPEVACEK**

American Folk Song

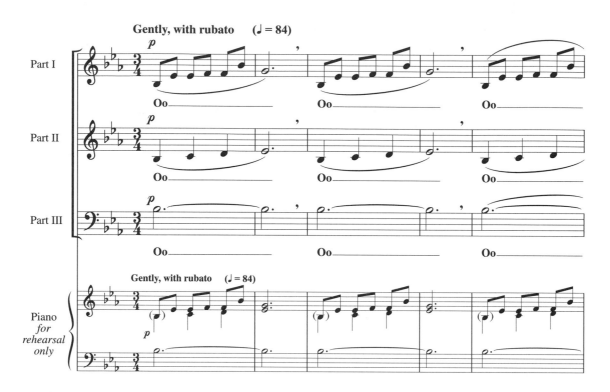

*Adjust text to fit choice of verses.

3. Build me a castle forty feet high.
So I can see him (her) as he (she) rides by.
As he (she) rides by, love, as he (she) rides by,
So I can see him (her) as he (she) rides by.

4. If you don't love me, love whom you please
Put your arms 'round me, give my heart ease.
Give my heart ease, love, give my heart ease.
Throw your arms 'round me, give my heart ease.

5. Write me a letter, send it by mail.
Send it in care of Birmingham jail.
Birmingham jail, love, Birmingham jail.
Send it in care of Birmingham jail.

Repeat first verse

Elijah Rock!

Composer: Traditional Spiritual, arranged by Roger Emerson
Text: Traditional
Voicing: 3-Part Mixed

VOCABULARY

syncopation

spiritual

minor scale

rest

 SKILL BUILDERS

To learn more about syncopation, see Intermediate Sight-Singing, page 126.

Focus

- Read and perform syncopated rhythms.
- Perform music that represents the African American spiritual.

Getting Started

When you hear music that has catchy rhythms and a strong beat, you might find yourself tapping your foot, nodding your head or snapping your fingers. This excitement in music is often caused by syncopation. **Syncopation** occurs when *the accent is moved from the strong beat to a weak beat or the weak portion of the beat.* As you sing "Elijah Rock!" listen for the syncopated rhythms.

◆ History and Culture

"Elijah Rock!" is an example of a spiritual. Part of the African American traditions are **spirituals,** *songs that are often based on biblical themes or stories and were first sung by African American slaves.* These spirituals were probably sung while the slaves were working in the fields, engaging in social activities, or participating in worship. Syncopation and complex rhythms are common features found in spirituals.

Arranger Roger Emerson has added unique features to this arrangement. The slow, pensive introduction is followed by the driving syncopated chorus. Repeated sections are used to build momentum to the rousing final note.

Links to Learning

◆ Theory

This arrangement of "Elijah Rock!" is in the key of G minor and is based on the G minor scale. A **minor scale** is *a scale that has* la *as its keynote or home tone.* To locate "G" on the piano, find any set of three black keys. "G" is the white key just below the middle black key. This scale uses the notes G, A, B♭, C, D, E♭, F, G. Using the keyboard below as a guide, play the G minor scale.

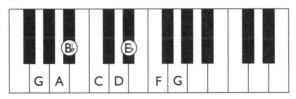

Syncopated rhythmic patterns sometimes contain rests. A **rest** is *a symbol used in music notation to indicate silence.* Read and perform the following example to practice shifting the accent from the strong beat to the weak portion of the beat. Find these patterns in the music.

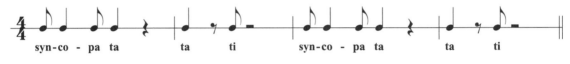

syn-co - pa ta   ta   ti   syn-co - pa ta   ta   ti

◆ Artistic Expression

Movement can enhance the interpretation or character of a song. Form two or more circles in the room. Walk to the beat of a drum. Once you are secure in walking the beat, begin singing "Elijah Rock!" Notice the words that fall on the beat and those that fall off the beat. This will help you discover where syncopation occurs in this song.

Evaluation

Demonstrate how well you have learned the skills and concepts featured in the lesson "Elijah Rock!" by completing the following:

- Alone or in a small group, sing measures 17–24 to show your ability to perform syncopated rhythms correctly. How well did you do?

- In what measures do the rests move the accent from the strong beat to the weak portion of the beat?

Elijah Rock!

For 3-Part Mixed and Piano

Adapted and Arranged by
ROGER EMERSON

Traditional Spiritual

*Optional: Add some Pt. II voices to top note

SPOTLIGHT

Diction

Singing is a form of communication. To communicate well while singing, you must not only form your vowels correctly, but also say your consonants as clearly and cleanly as possible.

There are two kinds of consonants: voiced and unvoiced. Consonants that require the use of the voice along with the **articulators** *(lips, teeth, tongue, and other parts of the mouth and throat)* are called voiced consonants. If you place your hand on your throat, you can actually feel your voice box vibrate while producing them. Unvoiced consonant sounds are made with the articulators only.

In each pair below, the first word contains a voiced consonant while the second word contains an unvoiced consonant. Speak the following word pairs, then sing them on any pitch. When singing, make sure the voiced consonant is on the same pitch as the vowel.

Voiced:	Unvoiced Consonants:	More Voiced Consonants:
[b] bay	[p] pay	[l] lip
[d] den	[t] ten	[m] mice
[g] goat	[k] coat	[n] nice
[ʤ] jeer	[ʧ] cheer	[j] yell
[z] zero	[s] scenic	[r] red
[ʒ] fusion	[ʃ] shun	
[ð] there	[θ] therapy	More Unvoiced Consonants:
[v] vine	[f] fine	[h] have
[w] wince	[hw] whim	

The American "r" requires special treatment in classical choral singing. To sing an American "r" at the end of a syllable following a vowel, sing the vowel with your teeth apart and jaw open. In some formal sacred music and English texts, you may need to flip or roll the "r." For most other instances, sing the "r" on pitch, then open to the following vowel quickly.

America The Beautiful

Composer: Samuel A. Ward, arranged by Joyce Eilers
Text: Katharine Lee Bates
Voicing: 3-Part Mixed

VOCABULARY

stage presence

legato

suspension

Focus

- Demonstrate musical artistry and appropriate performance practice.
- Describe suspension using music terminology.
- Identify the relationships between the other fine arts and those of music.

Getting Started

Choose the correct definition for the words listed below.

1. alabaster   **a.** magical saying   **b.** white granite
2. spacious   **a.** with lots of space   **b.** gracious
3. amber   **a.** a hot fire   **b.** golden in color
4. fruited plain   **a.** a nutty place   **b.** a field filled with fruit

Find these words in "America the Beautiful." Understanding the words helps you express the meaning of a song.

◆ History and Culture

In 1893, Katharine Lee Bates, a professor at Wellesley College in Massachusetts, traveled to Colorado to present a series of lectures. Upon viewing the Rocky Mountains for the very first time, Ms. Bates was overwhelmed. She had never seen such tall and majestic mountains. She hiked to the top of Pike's Peak, and as she looked over the wide, fertile land below, the opening lines of "America The Beautiful" came to her. The poem was first published on July 4, 1895, and was later put to music.

When you sing, your **stage presence** (*a performer's overall appearance on stage, including enthusiasm, facial expression and posture*) affects the outcome of the performance. An enthusiastic stage presence will show your audience how important singing about America is to you.

To learn more about singing posture, see page 35.

Links to Learning

◆ Vocal

Perform the following example to practice singing **legato** (*a connected and sustained style of singing*). A successful legato sound requires a constant and steady flow of air.

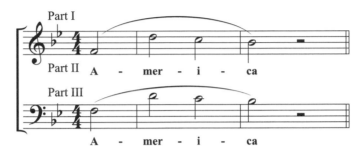

◆ Theory

Perform the three examples below to practice singing a suspension. A **suspension** is *the holding over of one or more musical tones of a chord into the following chord, producing a momentary discord*. In each example, Part III provides the suspended tone, which resolves downward (C to B♭, or *re* to *do*).

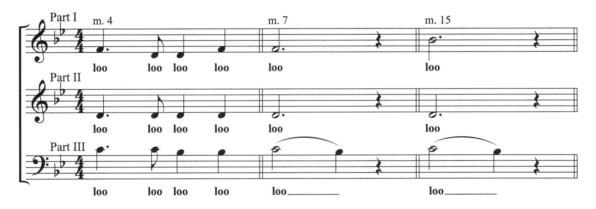

◆ Artistic Expression

Using colored pencils, crayons, or markers, create artwork that portrays an image or scene described in Katharine Lee Bates' poem.

Evaluation

Demonstrate how well you have learned the skills and concepts featured in the lesson "America The Beautiful" by completing the following:

- Sing measures 12–19 to show your ability to sing in a legato style.
- Listen to a recording of your choir singing measures 1–11 of "America The Beautiful." Raise your hand each time you hear Part III sing the suspension and its resolution.
- Share your artwork depicting a scene from "America The Beautiful" with the class. Explain what scene you chose to portray and why.

America The Beautiful

For 3-Part Mixed and Piano

Arranged by JOYCE EILERS

Words by KATHARINE LEE BATES
Music by SAMUEL A. WARD

crown thy good with broth - er-hood from sea to shin - ing sea.

crown thy good with broth - er-hood from sea to shin - ing sea.

crown thy good with broth - er-hood from sea to shin - ing sea.

NARRATOR: I am an American! I love my nation and my God, and I owe a debt to our forefathers who worked so hard and sacrificed so much to give

Soprano or unison* *p* 21

Oh beau - ti - ful for pil - grim feet, whose stern im - pas - sioned

*Pace the narration to end before measure 29

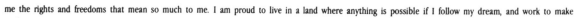

SPOTLIGHT

Posture

Posture is important for good singing. By having the body properly aligned, you are able to breathe correctly so that you have sufficient breath support needed to sing more expressively and for longer periods of time.

To experience, explore and establish proper posture for singing, try the following:

Standing

- Pretend someone is gently pulling up on a thread attached to the top of your head.
- Let out all of your air like a deflating balloon.
- Raise your arms up over your head.
- Take in a deep breath as if you were sipping through a straw.
- Slowly lower your arms down to your sides.
- Let all your air out on a breathy "pah," keeping your chest high.
- Both feet on floor, shoulder-width apart.
- Chest high, shoulders relaxed.
- Neck relaxed, head straight.

Sitting

- Sit on the edge of a chair with your feet flat on the floor while keeping your chest lifted.
- Hold your music with one hand and turn pages with the other.
- Always hold the music up so you can easily see the director and your music.

Cantemos Alleluia

Composer: Emily Crocker
Text: Based on Psalm 148
Voicing: SAB

VOCABULARY

concert etiquette

ABA form

descant

parallel sixths

Focus

- Identify and perform music in ABA form.
- Describe and perform parallel sixths.
- Interpret the text in an expressive manner.

 **SPOTLIGHT**

To learn more about concert etiquette, see page 99.

Getting Started

If you were to listen to a live performance of "Cantemos Alleluia," you would most likely respond enthusiastically to the energy and excitement of this song. But as an audience member, it is also your responsibility to respond appropriately. **Concert etiquette** is *a term used to describe how we are expected to behave in formal musical performances.* Participation in choir will help you become not only a better singer, but also a more appreciative audience member.

◆ History and Culture

"Cantemos Alleluia" is written in ABA form. **ABA form** is *the design in which the opening phrases (section A) are followed by contrasting phrases (section B), which leads to a repetition of the opening phrases (section A).* Section A of "Cantemos Alleluia" (measures 1–29) consists of two melodies. First, the Baritones sing a melody in English. Then, the Sopranos and Altos introduce a new melody in Spanish. Section B (measures 30–55) has a contrasting melody. When section A returns, composer Emily Crocker combines the English melody and the Spanish melody. The song's rousing ending includes a **descant,** or *a special part that is usually sung higher than the melody.* Find these sections in the music.

Links to Learning

◆ **Vocal**

Perform the following example to sing the word "Alleluia" with tall vowel sounds. Is this example most like the melody in section A or section B?

◆ **Theory**

Perform the following example to experience singing parallel sixths. **Parallel sixths** are *a group of notes that are a sixth apart and move in parallel motion.* Find the parallel sixths in section B.

◆ **Artistic Expression**

If you are not familiar with Spanish, memorize the English translation of the Spanish lyrics to this song. When singing in Spanish, think about the English translation so that you communicate the meaning of the text to your audience.

Evaluation

Demonstrate how well you have learned the skills and concepts featured in the lesson "Cantemos Alleluia" by completing the following:

• Make up simple motions to use while singing section A (swaying, tapping, clapping, etc.). Stand still during section B. To demonstrate your understanding of ABA form, perform the entire song moving or standing still during each section.

• Define *parallel sixths*. Find one example of parallel sixths in the music.

• Working with a partner, quiz each other's knowledge of the English translation for the Spanish lyrics.

For the 1993 TMEA Region 19 Jr. High Choir, Houston, Texas

Cantemos Alleluia

For SAB and Piano

Text based on
Psalm 148

Music by
EMILY CROCKER

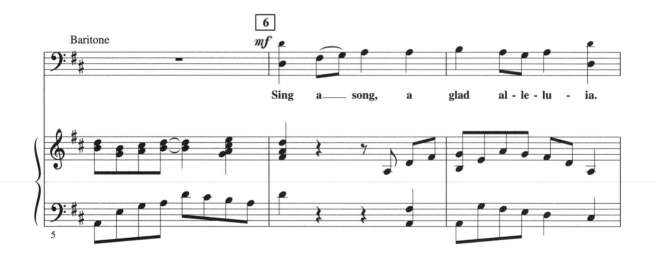

Sing a— song, a glad al-le-lu- ia.

Come and re-joice and sing to God.— Sing a— song, a

glad al‑le‑lu‑ia. Come and re‑joice and sing_____ to

Soprano

Alto

God.

17 Unis. *mf*

Can‑te‑mos

Sing now a

al‑le‑lu‑ia. Can‑te‑mos al Se‑ñor.____

glad al‑le‑lu‑ia. Sing now un‑to the Lord.

*Optional English lyrics

heights. Sing all ye an - gels, sun and moon, and

stars at night. Moun - tains, hills, and val - leys,

trees and crea-tures great and small, kings and peo - ple one and all,

sing un-to the Lord.

46 Unis.
mp

Can - te - mos   al - le-lu - ia,
Sing   now   your   al - le-lu - ias,

un can - ti - co   de amor.
sing   now   a   song   of love.

El   hi   zo el   cie - lo,   el
God   made   the   heav - ens,   the

mar,   el   sol,   y las es - tre - llas!
sea,   the   sun,   and all the   stars!

lu - ia, al - le - lu -

Come and re - joice and sing_____ to

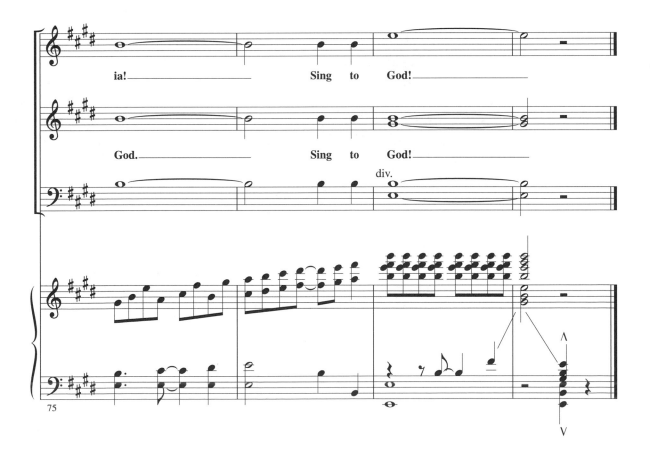

ia!_____ Sing to God!_____

God._____ Sing to God!_____

div.

Winter Storm

Composer: Audrey Snyder
Text: Audrey Snyder
Voicing: 3-Part Mixed

VOCABULARY
chord

syncopation

Focus

• Relate music to other subjects.

• Use standard terminology to describe a chord.

• Read and perform syncopated rhythmic patterns.

 **SKILL BUILDERS**

To learn more about the key of D minor, see Intermediate Sight-Singing, *page 52.*

Getting Started

Select one word to complete the following phrases.

1. *Who has seen the _____, neither you nor I, but when the leaves bow down their heads the _____ is passing by.*

2. The _____ chill factor today is a frigid -3°. Brrr!

The word is *wind*, the ubiquitous weather phenomenon present in every season. For such a small word, it can cause much havoc. Its strong force during a tornado or hurricane can destroy an entire house or region. In the winter, the wind can change a few inches of snow into a treacherous blizzard that paralyzes a community. *Wind*—a small word with a mighty punch.

◆ History and Culture

To prepare for this lesson, write an acrostic poem about the wind. An acrostic poem is one in which the first letter of each line, taken in order, forms a word. Write each letter of the word *wind* down the side of your paper. Then, compose a four-line poem with descriptive words that begin with each letter of the word *wind*. Study the example below to get started.

W *ailing and howling,*

I *ncessant and urgent,*

N *ovember winds blow*

D *ecember to calendar's end.*

Links to Learning

◆ **Vocal**

Perform the following example to sing chords that are used in "Winter Storm." A **chord** is *a combination of three or more notes sung at the same time.*

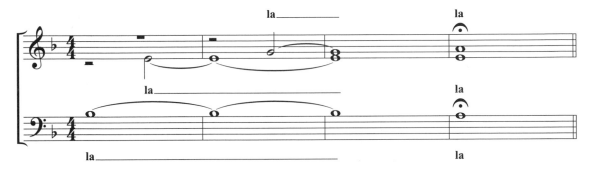

◆ **Theory**

Syncopation is *a rhythmic pattern in which the placement of accents is on a weak beat or a weak portion of the beat.* Copy the following rhythmic patterns on a sheet of paper. Perform by clapping, tapping or chanting. What makes these patterns syncopated?

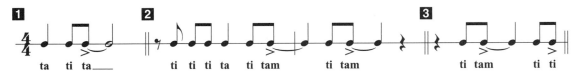

Evaluation

Demonstrate how well you have learned the skills and concepts featured in the lesson "Winter Storm" by completing the following:

- Share your acrostic poem with the class. Find places in the music that match the descriptive words you used in your poem.

- With a partner, perform measures 10–17 to show your ability to sing syncopated rhythms correctly. One partner will tap steady eighth notes while the other partner sings. Switch roles. How did you do?

Winter Storm

from *Windseasons*

For 3-Part Mixed and Piano

Words and Music by
AUDREY SNYDER

the bit-ter wind comes rac - ing forth,__ First, whirl-ing gusts and swirl-

sim.

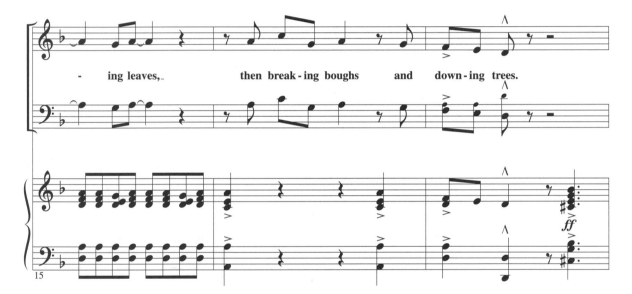

- ing leaves,__ then break-ing boughs and down-ing trees.

ff

The surg-ing tide and churn - ing sea,__ the crash-ing waves are rush-

mp

ing free,___ The foam-y o - cean pounds___ the rocks;___

it jumps the road and floods the side - walks.

Blast and blow, re - lent-less gale,___ rage and roar in squall and squail.___

sub. *mp*

pound-ing doors and rat - t'ling sash - es.   Na-ture tru - ly owns___ the hour,___

with rug - ged force   and   awe-some pow'r.   The cra - zy wheel - ing weath -

Ah

- er vane,___   win - dows drenched   with   driv - ing rain,___

Ah
Unis.
hum - ble shel - ter 'gainst the storm,
yet here in - side we're safe and
mf
53
f
warm!
59
Blast and blow, re - lent - less gale,
f sub. mp
57
'Round the hous - es whine and
rage and roar in squall and squail.
Ah and
61

SPOTLIGHT

Vowels

The style of a given piece of music dictates how we should pronounce the words. If we are singing a more formal, classical piece, then we need to form taller vowels as in very proper English. If we are singing in a jazz or pop style, then we should pronounce the words in a more relaxed, conversational way. To get the feeling of taller vowels for classical singing, do the following:

- Let your jaw gently drop down and back as if it were on a hinge.

- Place your hands on your cheeks beside the corners of your mouth.

- Sigh on an *ah* [a] vowel sound, but do not spread the corners of your mouth.

- Now sigh on other vowel sounds—*eh* [ɛ], *ee* [i], *oh* [o] and *oo* [u]—keeping the back of the tongue relaxed.

- As your voice goes from higher notes to lower notes, think of gently opening a tiny umbrella inside your mouth.

ee	eh or ā*	ah	oh	oo
[i]	[ɛ] [e]	[a]	[o]	[u]

Other vowel sounds used in singing are diphthongs. A **diphthong** is *a combination of two vowel sounds.* For example, the vowel *ay* consists of two sounds: *eh* [E] and *ee* [i]. To sing a diphthong correctly, stay on the first vowel sound for the entire length of the note, only lightly adding the second vowel sound as you move to another note or lift off the note.

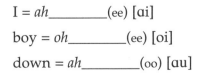

I = *ah*_____(ee) [ɑi]

boy = *oh*_____(ee) [oi]

down = *ah*_____(oo) [ɑu]

*Note: This is an Italian "ā," which is one sound, and not an American "ā," which is a diphthong, or two sounds.

Shalom Aleichem

Composer: I. and S. E. Goldfarb, arranged by Gil Aldema, edited by J. Mark Dunn
Text: Traditional
Voicing: SAB

VOCABULARY

articulation

staccato

legato

harmonic minor
   scale

Focus

- Sing music using various articulation styles.
- Write and perform music in the key of A minor.
- Perform music that represents the Jewish culture.

Getting Started

Match the following greetings with the correct country.

1.	*bonjour*	**a.**	Italy
2.	*konnichi wa*	**b.**	Spain
3.	*ssalamu 'lekum*	**c.**	Japan
4.	*ciao*	**d.**	Israel
5.	*hola*	**e.**	France
6.	*shalom*	**f.**	Morocco

It is not uncommon for greetings to have more than one meaning. For example, the Hebrew greeting *shalom* means "hello," "goodbye" and "peace."

◆ History and Culture

Shalom aleichem, (translated, "Peace be with you") is a traditional Hebrew greeting that Jewish families sing at Shabbat (Sabbath) on Friday evenings. The Hebrew words and Yiddish melody welcome the Shabbat angels to the dinner table and wish them a safe journey back home. Candles are always present at the Shabbat table, but there can also be fresh flowers, handmade paper decorations and challah—a special braided egg bread—to celebrate the peace and joy of the occasion.

The Shabbat spirit of togetherness is also reflected in this beautiful arrangement of "Shalom Aleichem." The vocal lines intertwine and complement each other with musical sensitivity. Listen carefully while you sing and decide how you can support the others in your choir by using dynamic contrast and expressive phrasing.

 **SKILL BUILDERS**

To learn more about the A harmonic minor scale, see Intermediate Sight-Singing, page 68.

Links to Learning

◆ Vocal

Articulation is *the amount of separation or connection between notes.* Perform the following example **staccato** (*a short and detached style of singing*). Then, sing it again **legato** (*a connected and sustained style of singing*), disregarding the staccato markings. When singing legato, use lots of breath support on the syllable "-lom" to avoid an aspirated "h" sound between pitches.

◆ Theory

"Shalom Aleichem" is loosely based on the harmonic minor scale. The **harmonic minor scale** is *a minor scale in which the* sol *(7th pitch) is raised a half step to* si. Sing the following A harmonic minor scale.

Evaluation

Demonstrate how well you have learned the skills and concepts featured in the lesson "Shalom Aleichem" by completing the following:

- Choose a four-measure phrase from "Shalom Aleichem" to sing for a classmate. Sing the phrase first in a staccato style and then in a legato style. Switch roles. Evaluate how well you were able to sing in both styles.

- Using the pitches found in the A harmonic minor scale, compose a four-measure melody in $\frac{4}{4}$ meter that begins and ends on *la* or A. Perform your melody for the class. Check your work for rhythmic and melodic accuracy.

Shalom Aleichem

For SAB, a cappella

Arranged by GIL ALDEMA
Edited by J. MARK DUNN

Music by
I. & S. E. GOLDFARB

Peace be to you, messengers of peace

angels of the Most High

who is Ruler of rulers

the Holy and Blessed One.

Come to us in peace...
Bless us with peace...

Depart in peace...

S: mal - chei ham'-la - chim ha - ka-dosh ba - ruch__ hu.

A: ham' - la - chim ha - ka-dosh ba-ruch hu.

B: ham' - - la - - - chim ha - ka-dosh ba-ruch hu.

SPOTLIGHT

Arranging

In music, an **arrangement** is *a composition in which a composer takes an existing melody and adds extra features or changes the melody in some way.* An **arranger** is *a composer who writes an arrangement by changing an existing melody to fit certain musical parameters.* The arranger has the following things to consider:

- Pitch—What is the range of the melody?

- Tempo—What is the speed of the beat?

- Instrumentation—Is the music for voices, instruments or both?

- Accompaniment—What will be used for accompaniment (piano, guitar, etc.), if anything?

- Harmony—What type of chords will be used for the harmony?

- Melody/Countermelody—Will harmony be added by use of a **countermelody** (*a separate vocal line that supports and contrasts the primary melody*)?

Read and perform the familiar melody "Hot Cross Buns."

Now you are ready to write your own arrangement. Using "Hot Cross Buns" as the existing melody, decide which element or elements you wish to change to compose your arrangement. You can try one or more of the ideas listed below:

- Pitch—Start the song higher or lower than currently written.

- Tempo—Alter the tempo in some manner (faster or slower).

- Instrumentation—Play the melody on different instruments.

- Accompaniment—Use a piano, guitar or other instrument to accompany your melody.

- Harmony—Add harmony notes from the chords and play them on an instrument or sing them with the melody.

- Melody/Countermelody—Compose a second melody or countermelody that fits musically with the existing melody.

Calypso Gloria

Composer: Emily Crocker
Text: Traditional Latin
Voicing: SATB

VOCABULARY

calypso

diction

syncopation

SPOTLIGHT

To learn more about diction, see page 25.

Focus

- Sing in Latin using tall, pure vowel sounds.
- Perform music that contains calypso rhythms.
- Create and perform rhythmic phrases.

Getting Started

Have you ever seen a parade? Maybe you have watched the Macy's Thanksgiving Day Parade from New York City, or the Rose Bowl Parade from Pasadena, California. At first, you can hear the music of the marching band long before you can see it. The sound is distant. As the band moves closer and closer, the sound gets louder and louder. Then, it passes by in full display. Soon the band marches on and the sound fades away. When you perform "Calypso Gloria," think of the passing band and the changing dynamics from beginning to end.

◆ History and Culture

Calypso is *a style of music that originated in the West Indies and which features syncopated rhythms.* Composer Emily Crocker has taken the syncopated rhythms associated with calypso music and used them in "Calypso Gloria." The calypso style of music can be traced back to the early slaves in the Caribbean islands of Trinidad and Tobago. During that time, slaves were forbidden to speak to one another. They developed a unique way of communicating through singing. From this the rhythms of calypso music emerged, a blend of African, Spanish and French influence.

The translation of the Latin text is as follows:

Gloria in excelsis deo. Et in terra pax hominibus bonae voluntatis.

Glory to God on high. And on earth peace to men of good will.

Links to Learning

◆ Vocal

As you perform the example below, let your jaw gently drop down and back as if it were on a hinge. Place your hands on your cheeks beside the corners of your mouth. Sing this example at a very slow tempo. **Diction,** or *the pronunciation of words while singing,* includes both tall, pure vowels and crisp consonants.

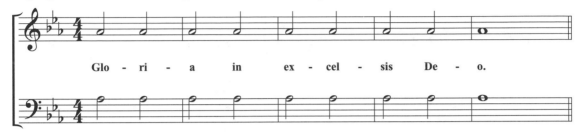

Glo - ri - a in ex - cel - sis De - o.

◆ Theory

Syncopation is *a rhythmic pattern that places the accents on a weak beat or a weak portion of the beat.* Read and perform the following examples to practice placing the accents off the beat.

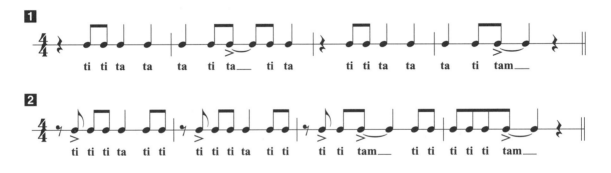

◆ Artistic Expression

To develop artistry through movement, clap the rhythmic patterns in the Theory section above while stepping the steady beat. For a super challenge, clap the steady beat while you step the syncopated rhythms!

Evaluation

Demonstrate how well you have learned the skills and concepts featured in the lesson "Calypso Gloria" by completing the following:

- Record yourself as you sing measures 29–36. Listen carefully to the recording and evaluate how well you were able to sing with pure, tall vowel sounds.

- Accompany your choir as they sing "Calypso Gloria." Play Example 1 from the Theory section above using hand percussion instruments such as finger cymbals, a guiro, rhythm sticks, a tambourine or a hand drum.

- Write an original four-measure rhythmic phrase that contains syncopation. Perform your phrase for another student. Check your work for rhythmic accuracy and the correct notation for syncopation.

Calypso Gloria

For SATB and Piano with Optional Bass and Percussion*

Traditional Latin

Music by EMILY CROCKER

* Pizz. bass may double piano LH

SPOTLIGHT

Pitch Matching

As you begin to learn how to read music, you must learn not only how to identify the notes on the printed page, but also how to sing the notes you read in tune. Accurate pitch matching requires that you hear the note in your head before you sing it instead of trying to find the note with your voice. Learning to sing from one note to another in scale patterns will help you hear the notes in your head before you sing them. Perform the scale below first using note names, then numbers, and finally solfège syllables.

C	D	E	F	G	A	B	C	B	A	G	F	E	D	C
1	2	3	4	5	6	7	8	7	6	5	4	3	2	1
do	re	mi	fa	sol	la	ti	do	ti	la	sol	fa	mi	re	do

To help you sing the following examples on the correct pitch, hear the notes in your head before you sing them. If you cannot hear the interval skip in your head before you sing it, mentally sing the first note followed by all the notes in between until you come to the right note. Then, begin again and sing the pattern as written.

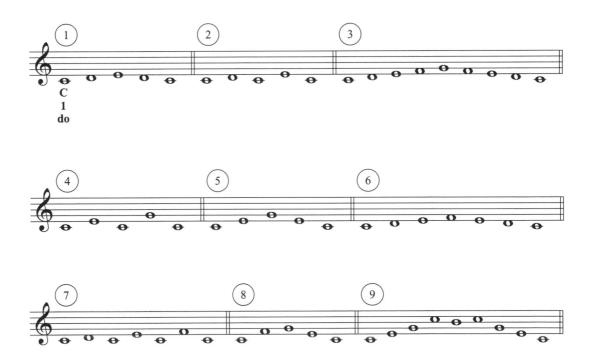

Innsbruck, ich muss dich lassen

Composer: Heinrich Isaac (c. 1450–1517), edited by John Leavitt
Text: Heinrich Isaac
Voicing: SATB

VOCABULARY

Renaissance period

motet

madrigal

$\frac{3}{2}$ meter

$\frac{2}{2}$ meter

MUSIC & HISTORY

To learn more about the Renaissance period, see page 108.

Focus

- Describe and perform music from the Renaissance period.
- Read and write music in $\frac{3}{2}$ meter and $\frac{2}{2}$ meter.

Getting Started

If composer Heinrich Isaac lived today, he would probably take skis and a snowboard to Innsbruck, because this beautiful Austrian town is nestled among the snow-capped Alps. When Isaac arrived in Innsbruck around 1500, however, he probably brought musical instruments, parchment and feather pens. That's because Maximilian I, the Holy Roman Emperor, had persuaded Isaac to leave Florence, Italy, and come to Innsbruck to serve as an imperial diplomat and court composer. Isaac is best remembered for his German song "Innsbruck, ich muss dich lassen."

◆ History and Culture

Heinrich Isaac (c. 1450–1517) lived during the **Renaissance period** *(1430–1600)*. Vocal music flourished during the Renaissance. The short pieces that composers wrote for singers fall into two categories, the motet and the madrigal. A **motet** is *a short, sacred choral piece with Latin text that is used in religious services but is not a part of the regular mass.* A **madrigal** is *a short, secular choral piece of the Renaissance period with text in the common language.* The joys and sorrows of love are common themes for madrigals, as are stories of country life. As a rule, most motets and madrigals are unaccompanied. Although "Innsbruck, ich muss dich lassen" ("Innsbruck, I Now Must Leave You") has a German text, Isaac used several characteristics of the Italian madrigal in this piece.

Links to Learning

◆ Vocal

"Innsbruck, ich muss dich lassen" is in the key of G major and is based on the G major scale. To locate "G" on the keyboard, find any set of three black keys. "G" is the white key just to the left of the middle black key. This scale uses the notes G, A, B, C, D, E, F#, G. Using the keyboard as a guide, play the G major scale.

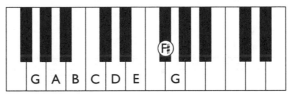

Sing the G major scale.

◆ Theory

This song is written in $\frac{3}{2}$ **meter** (*a time signature in which there are three beats per measure and the half note receives the beat*) and in $\frac{2}{2}$ **meter** (*a time signature in which there are two beats per measure and the half note receives the beat*). Perform the following example to practice reading rhythmic patterns in both of these meters.

Evaluation

Demonstrate how well you have learned the skills and concepts featured in the lesson "Innsbruck, ich muss dich lassen" by completing the following:

- Discuss the musical characteristics of the Renaissance period.

- Using the music as a guide, compose a four-measure rhythmic pattern in $\frac{3}{2}$ or $\frac{2}{2}$ meter. Play your pattern on a rhythm instrument for the class. Check your work for correct use of notation and rhythms in $\frac{3}{2}$ or $\frac{2}{2}$ meter.

Innsbruck, ich muss dich lassen
(Innsbruck, I Now Must Leave You)

For SATB, a cappella

Edited with English text by
JOHN LEAVITT

HEINRICH ISAAC
(c. 1450–1517)

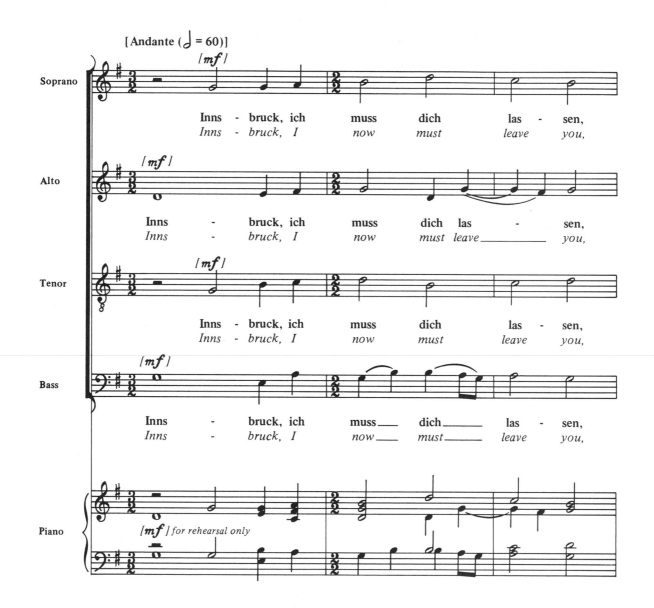

SPOTLIGHT

Breath Management

Vocal sound is produced by air flowing between the vocal cords; therefore, correct breathing is important for good singing. Good breath management provides you with the support needed to sing expressively and for longer periods of time.

To experience, explore and establish proper breathing for singing, try the following:

- Put your hands on your waist at the bottom of your rib cage.

- Take in an easy breath for four counts, as if through a straw, without lifting your chest or shoulders.

- Feel your waist and rib cage expand all the way around like an inflating inner tube.

- Let your breath out slowly on "sss," feeling your "inner tube" deflating as if it has a slow leak.

- Remember to keep your chest up the entire time.

- Take in another easy breath for four counts before your "inner tube" has completely deflated, then let your air out on "sss" for eight counts.

- Repeat this step several times, taking in an easy breath for four counts and gradually increasing the number of counts to let your air out to sixteen counts.

Sometimes in singing it is necessary to take a quick or "catch" breath.

- Look out the window and imagine seeing something wonderful for the first time, like snow.

- Point your finger at the imaginary something and let in a quick, silent breath that expresses your wonderment and surprise.

- A quick breath is not a gasping breath, but rather a silent breath.

Come Joyfully Sing

Composer: George Frideric Handel (1685–1759), edited by Patrick M. Liebergen
Text: English text by Patrick M. Liebergen
Voicing: SAB

VOCABULARY

Baroque period

oratorio

serenata

dynamics

conductor

MUSIC & HISTORY

*To learn more about the
Baroque period,
see page 112.*

Focus

• Describe and perform music from the Baroque period.

• Perform music with accurate dynamics.

• Read and conduct rhythmic patterns in $\frac{3}{4}$ meter.

Getting Started

If you attended a wedding in 1708, you might have heard "Come Joyfully Sing," instead of "Here Comes the Bride." That is because "Come Joyfully Sing" was written for a wedding celebration. During the eighteenth century, it was not uncommon for composers to write music for special occasions such as weddings and birthdays for members of the royal family.

◆ History and Culture

George Frideric Handel (1685–1759) is one of the most famous composers from the **Baroque period** *(1600–1750)*. Born in Germany, he studied harpsichord, oboe, organ and violin and began composing at a young age. As an adult, he lived and worked in Italy and England, where he composed operas and other works. One of his most famous compositions is the "Hallelujah Chorus" from an **oratorio** *(a dramatic work for solo voices, chorus and orchestra presented without theatrical action)* called the *Messiah*.

"Come Joyfully Sing" was composed in 1708 and is from a larger work called a **serenata,** or *a dramatic cantata or semi-opera written for a special occasion*. A serenata differs from a full-scale opera in that the singers are stationary and do not move about the stage. "Come Joyfully Sing" is from Handel's serenata *Acis, Galatea, e Polifemo* that tells the mythological tale of Acis (a shepherd), Galatea (a sea nymph), and Polifemo (a cyclops). Serenatas were very popular during the Baroque period.

Links to Learning

◆ Vocal

Using solfege syllables, perform the following example to practice good intonation in the key of B♭ major. Notice the contrasting **dynamics,** or *symbols that indicate how loud or soft to sing,* and follow these as you sing.

◆ Theory

Conducting is an important part of musical performance. A **conductor** is *a person who uses hand and arm gestures to interpret the expressive elements of music for singers and instrumentalists.*

Read and perform the following examples to practice rhythmic patterns in $\frac{3}{4}$ meter. Conduct the $\frac{3}{4}$ pattern as you count the patterns below. Start with a moderate to slow tempo. Repeat the pattern several times, each time using a different tempo. As the tempo increases, you will start feeling the beat in one rather than in three.

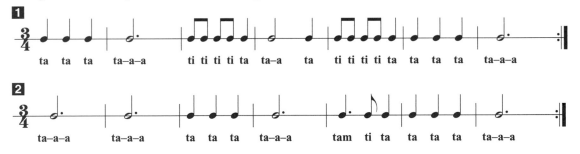

Evaluation

Demonstrate how well you have learned the skills and concepts featured in the lesson "Come Joyfully Sing" by completing the following:

• Discuss the musical characteristics of the Baroque period.

• Sing measures 30–45 in a group of six (two to a part), accurately following all dynamics. Discuss as a group how well you were able to show the varied dynamics.

• Be a conductor! Conduct the choir singing measures 1–13 of "Come Joyfully Sing." First, establish a moderate tempo and appropriate conducting pattern. Then, repeat at the performance tempo with the correct conducting pattern. Can you successfully conduct in patterns of one and three?

Come Joyfully Sing

For SAB and Piano

Arranged with English Text by
PATRICK M. LIEBERGEN

GEORGE FRIDERIC HANDEL
(1685–1759)

joy we sing; plea - sure to you we bring!

joy we sing; plea - sure to you we bring!

joy we sing; plea - sure to you we bring!

32

Come, come sing we to - geth - er; come and

Come, come sing we to - geth - er; come and

Come, come sing we to - geth - er; come and

38

come   joy - ful - ly   sing;   let   your   voic   -   es,

come   joy - ful - ly   sing;   let   your   voic   -   es,

come   joy - ful - ly   sing;   let   your   voic   -   es,

voic - es   now   ring!

voic - es   now _ ring!

voic - es   now   ring!

Bless The Lord, O My Soul

Composer: Mikhail Ippolitov-Ivanov (1859–1935), edited by Joyce Eilers
Text: Psalm 103
Voicing: 3-Part Mixed

VOCABULARY

syncopation

Romantic period

dynamic markings

tempo markings

MUSIC & HISTORY

To learn more about the Romantic period, see page 120.

Focus

• Read, write and perform rhythmic patterns with syncopation.

• Read and perform music in the key of E♭ major.

• Describe and perform music from the Romantic period.

Getting Started

Composers often show the importance of different words in a song's text with clever notation tactics. Often, various dynamics and rhythms are used to accomplish this. In "Bless The Lord, O My Soul," both are used extensively. The song features many contrasts in dynamics. **Syncopation,** or *the intentional placement of an accent on a weak beat or weak portion of the beat,* is used throughout this song to emphasize words of importance. Notice how the composer rhythmically places the word *bless* in the text. As you learn "Bless The Lord, O My Soul," challenge yourself to perform this song freely and expressively.

◆ History and Culture

Mikhail Ippolitov-Ivanov (1859–1935) was a composer and teacher. Born in Russia, he lived and worked during the **Romantic period** *(1820–1900).* He studied music at the St. Petersburg Conservatory and later in life taught at the Moscow Conservatory. In addition, he was the director of the Russian Choral Society.

Though primarily a composer of orchestral music and operas, Ippolitov-Ivanov wrote a variety of short choral pieces. "Bless The Lord, O My Soul" is one of these works. With its singable melody and full sound, this song is an example of the choral music of the Romantic period.

Links to Learning

◆ Vocal

"Bless The Lord, O My Soul" is in the key of E♭ major and is based on the E♭ major scale. To locate "E♭" on the piano, find any set of two black keys. "E♭" is the black key on the right. This scale uses the notes E♭, F, G, A♭, B♭, C, D, E♭. Using the keyboard below as a guide, play the E♭ major scale.

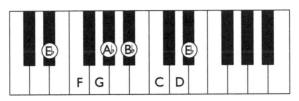

Sing the E♭ major scale.

◆ Theory

Read and perform the following examples to practice rhythmic patterns that use syncopation.

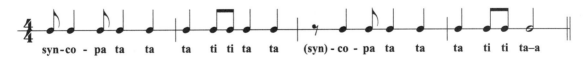

◆ Artistic Expression

By adhering to the **dynamic markings** (*symbols in music that indicate how loud or soft to sing*) and the **tempo markings** (*terms in music that indicate how fast or slow to sing*) found in the score of the music, you will add artistic expression to your performance.

Evaluation

Demonstrate how well you have learned the skills and concepts featured in the lesson "Bless The Lord, O My Soul" by completing the following:

- Compose a four-measure rhythmic phrase that uses syncopation. You may want to use your music as a guide. Perform your phrase for the class.

- Sight-sing measures 25–32 to show your ability to read music in the key of E♭ major.

Bless The Lord, O My Soul

For 3-Part Mixed, a cappella

From Psalm 103
Edited by JOYCE EILERS

MIKHAIL IPPOLITOV-IVANOV
(1859–1935)

*Use for rehearsal purposes only, to reinforce tonality.

Lord and for-get __ not all His __ ben - e - fits. __ Bless the

Lord and for-get not all His ben - e - fits. __ Bless the

Lord and for-get __ not all His ben - e - fits. __ Bless the

Lord, __ O __ my soul, and all that is with-in me, bless His

Lord, __ O __ my soul, and all that is with-in me, bless His

Lord, __ O __ my soul, and all that is with-in me, bless His

O _____ my soul, and all that is with-in me bless His

O _____ my soul, and all that is with-in me bless His

O _____ my soul, and all that is with-in me bless His

30 Adagio

ho - ly name.____ Bless-ed art Thou,____ O ____ Lord.

ho - ly name.____ Bless-ed art Thou,____ O ____ Lord.

ho - ly name.____ Bless-ed art Thou,____ O ____ Lord.

30 Adagio

SPOTLIGHT

Concert Etiquette

The term **concert etiquette** describes *how we are expected to behave in formal musical performances.* Understanding appropriate concert etiquette allows you to be considerate of others, including audience members and performers. It also helps everyone attending to enjoy the performance.

Different types of musical performances dictate certain behavior guidelines. How one shows excitement at a rock concert is certainly worlds apart from the appropriate behavior at a formal concert or theater production. Understanding these differences allows audience members to behave in a manner that shows consideration and respect for everyone involved.

What are the expectations of a good audience member at a formal musical presentation?

- Arrive on time. If you arrive after the performance has begun, wait outside the auditorium until a break in the music to enter the hall.

- Remain quiet and still during the performance. Talking and moving around prevent others from hearing and enjoying the performance.

- Leave the auditorium only in case of an emergency. Try to leave during a break in the musical selections.

- Sing or clap along only when invited to do so by the performers or the conductor.

- Applaud at the end of a composition or when the conductor's arms are lowered at the conclusion of a performance. It is customary to not applaud between movements or sections of a major work.

- Save shouting, whistling and dancing for rock concerts or athletic events. These are never appropriate at formal musical performances.

Remembering these important behavior guidelines will ensure that everyone enjoys the show!

Sing To The Lord

Composer: Noel Goemanne (b. 1927)
Text: Based on the Psalms
Voicing: SATB

VOCABULARY

Contemporary
  period

mixed meter

sempre accel.

accent

MUSIC&HISTORY

*To learn more about the
Contemporary period,
see page 124.*

Focus

- Perform music in mixed meter.

- Identify musical symbols.

- Perform music that represents the Contemporary period.

Getting Started

For centuries, composers have used unusual rhythmic patterns to make a piece of music come alive for the singer and for the audience. In "Sing To The Lord," composer Noel Goemanne frequently changes from $\frac{3}{8}$ meter to $\frac{3}{4}$ meter to generate an energetic and dancelike style. "Sing To The Lord" is from his set of songs called *Three Meditations*.

◆ History and Culture

"Sing To The Lord" is a musical composition from the **Contemporary period** *(1900–present).* One common practice in this period was to compose music in **mixed meter,** *a technique in which the time signature changes frequently within a piece.* Look at the music. How many different time signatures can you find?

Noel Goemanne (b. 1927) was born and raised in Belgium, where his name is pronounced "Whoo-MAHN." Following more study in Europe, he migrated to the United States and settled in Dallas, Texas. There he continued his musical career with an extensive church music ministry and the publication of over three hundred compositions. In 1987, in honor of the Pope's visit to Texas, Goemanne was commissioned to compose the processional for the Papal Mass. *Fanfare and Concertato on "All Creatures of Our God and King"* was the result.

Links to Learning

◆ Vocal

To communicate well while singing, you must not only form your vowels correctly, but also voice your consonants as clearly and cleanly as possible with accurate and precise pitch. Perform the following exercise to develop crisp diction by singing first on "loo," and then on words.

◆ Theory

The rhythmic challenges found in this piece can be easily mastered by maintaining an even eighth-note pulse. Divide each quarter note into two steady eighth-note pulses. This technique will help you with the changes in meter. Keep the eighth note constant throughout the example. Stress the syllables indicated with an accent mark.

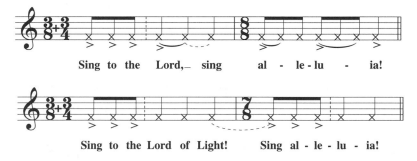

◆ Artistic Expression

In "Sing To The Lord," the term **sempre accel. (accelerando)** is *a marking that indicates to gradually get faster* and is used to bring the piece to an energetic closing. **Accents,** the *symbols placed above or below notes to indicate that those notes should receive extra emphasis or stress,* are also used. Find accents in the music and apply them to your performance.

Evaluation

Demonstrate how well you have learned the skills and concepts featured in the lesson "Sing To The Lord" by completing the following:

- Alone or in a small group, sing page 104 of the music to demonstrate rhythmic precision in mixed meter. Evaluate how well you did.

- Chant the last three measures of "Sing To The Lord" in rhythm and include the application of accents and sempre accel. as indicated. Were you able to demonstrate both while singing?

Sing To The Lord
from *Three Meditations*

For SATB and Piano

Based on the Psalms

Music by
NOEL GOEMANNE

high - est moun - tain - top; Sing to the Lord,___ pro - claim___ His Name!

marcato - - - - - - - -

S.

A.

T.

T. & B. *unis.*

B.

Sing to the Lord,___ sing al - le - lu - ia!

sempre accel.

'sing al - le - lu - ia; Sing, ___ O sing, ___ O sing, ___ O sing to the

sing al - le - lu - ia; Sing, ___ O sing, ___ O sing, ___ O sing to the

sempre accel. e crescendo

(L.H. legato)

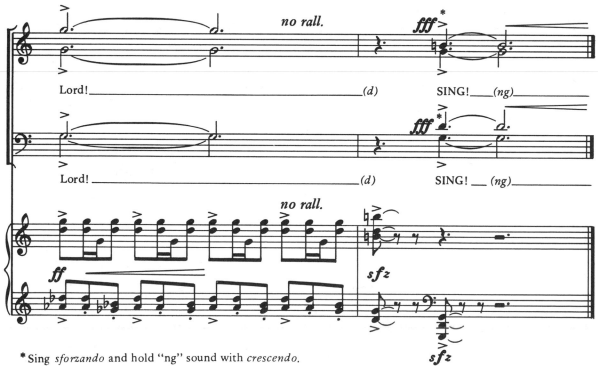

no rall.

Lord! _____ (d) SING! ___ (ng) _____

Lord! _____ (d) SING! ___ (ng) _____

no rall.

*Sing *sforzando* and hold "ng" sound with *crescendo.*

Music & History

Links to Music

Renaissance Period 108

    Innsbruck, ich muss dich lassen 78

Baroque Period 112

    Come Joyfully Sing 84

Classical Period 116

    Rise Up This Day To Celebrate 2

Romantic Period 120

    Bless The Lord, O My Soul 92

Contemporary Period 124

    Sing To The Lord 100

Sandro Botticelli (1445–1510) was an Italian painter who lived and worked in Florence, Italy, during the Renaissance. *The Adoration of the Magi* reflects the Renaissance interest in religious subjects. Framing the central figures within the strong geometric pillars emphasized those figures over others. Botticelli was also commissioned by the Pope to paint frescoes in the Sistine Chapel in the Vatican.

Sandro Botticelli. *The Adoration of the Magi.* c. 1480. Tempera and oil on panel. 70.2 x 104.2 cm (27 5/8 x 41"). National Gallery of Art, Washington, D. C. Andrew W. Mellon Collection.

Focus

- Describe the Renaissance period, including important developments.
- Describe characteristics of Renaissance music.

The Renaissance— A Time of Exploration

The **Renaissance period** *(1430–1600)* was a time during the fifteenth and sixteenth centuries of rapid development in exploration, science, art and music. This period could be called the beginning of modern history and the beginning of Western civilization as we know it now.

The development and use of the compass as a navigational aid in China made it possible for explorers to travel to new continents and to discover other cultures. Renaissance sailors first took to the seas to supply Europeans with Asian spices such as peppercorns, nutmeg and cinnamon. Also from the East came precious jewels and fine silk, a fabric especially valued for women's clothing.

Sailors also brought back information and customs from other cultures. This new information, along with a revived interest in writings from the ancient Greek and Roman cultures, was quickly spread across Europe, thanks to the invention of the printing press and mass-produced books. The invention of the printing press, credited to Johann Gutenberg, was one of the most significant developments of the Renaissance. As books became more available and less expensive, more people learned to read and began to consider new ideas.

A major change in the Christian religion occurred at this time. During the Protestant Reformation, various groups of Christians left the Catholic Church and formed some of the present-day Protestant denominations. Many Protestant groups translated Bibles from the Catholic Church's language of Latin to the language spoken by the people.

Remarkable advances were made in the arts and sciences by:

- Thomas Weelkes—English composer
- Gerardus Mercator—German mapmaker
- Vasco da Gama—Portuguese explorer who rounded the Horn of Africa and went on to India

COMPOSERS

Josquin des Prez
(c. 1450–1521)

Andrea Gabrieli
(c. 1510–1586)

Michael Praetorius
(1571–1621)

Thomas Weelkes
(c. 1576–1623)

ARTISTS

Gentile Bellini
(1429–1507)

Sandro Botticelli
(1445–1510)

Leonardo da Vinci
(1452–1519)

Michelangelo
(1475–1564)

Raphael
(1483–1520)

AUTHORS

Martin Luther
(1483–1546)

William Shakespeare
(1565–1616)

VOCABULARY

Renaissance period

sacred music

mass

motet

secular music

lute

polyphony

a cappella

madrigal

word painting

Renaissance Music

During the Renaissance, the Catholic Church gradually lost some of its influence over the daily lives of people. Much of the important music of the period, however, was still **sacred music**, or *music associated with religious services and themes*. In music, a **mass** is *a religious service of prayers and ceremonies*. A **motet** is *a shorter choral work, also set to a Latin text and used in religious services, but not part of the regular mass*. These two types of compositions were the most important forms of sacred Renaissance music. In Protestant churches, sacred music was composed and sung in the languages of the worshippers.

Like sacred music, **secular music**, or *music not associated with religious services or themes*, flourished during the Renaissance period. The center of musical activity gradually began to shift from churches to castles and towns. Music became an important form of entertainment for members of the emerging middle class. Social dancing became more widespread. Dance music of this period was written for **lute**, *an early form of the guitar*, and other instruments.

The Renaissance period is often referred to as the "golden age of polyphony." **Polyphony**, which literally means "many-sounding," is *a type of music in which there are two or more different melodic lines being sung or played at the same time*. Much of the choral music of the time was polyphonic, with as many as sixteen different vocal parts. Instruments were sometimes used to accompany and echo the voices.

Performance Links

When performing music of the Renaissance period, it is important to apply the following guidelines:

- Sing with clarity and purity of tone.
- Balance the vocal lines with equal importance.
- In polyphonic music, sing the rhythms accurately and with precision.
- When designated by the composer, sing **a cappella** (*unaccompanied or without instruments*).

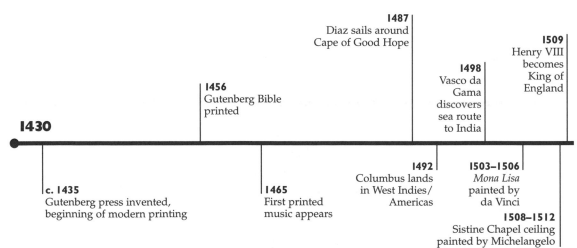

1487
Diaz sails around
Cape of Good Hope

1509
Henry VIII
becomes
King of
England

1498
Vasco da
Gama
discovers
sea route
to India

1456
Gutenberg Bible
printed

1430

c. 1435
Gutenberg press invented,
beginning of modern printing

1465
First printed
music appears

1492
Columbus lands
in West Indies/
Americas

1503–1506
Mona Lisa
painted by
da Vinci

1508–1512
Sistine Chapel ceiling
painted by Michelangelo

Listening Links

CHORAL SELECTION
"As Vesta Was Descending" by Thomas Weelkes (c.1576–1623)

Thomas Weelkes was an important English composer and organist. "As Vesta Was Descending" is an outstanding example of a **madrigal**, *a musical setting of a poem in three or more parts*. Generally, a madrigal has a secular text and is sung a cappella. This madrigal was written in honor of Queen Elizabeth I of England. This piece is an excellent example of **word painting**, *a technique in which the music reflects the meaning of the words*. Listen carefully to discover what occurs in the music on the following words: "descending," "ascending," "running down amain," "two by two," "three by three," and "all alone." Why do you think Weelkes chose to use the repeated text at the end?

INSTRUMENTAL SELECTION
"Three Voltas" from *Terpsichore* by Michael Praetorius (1571–1621)

During the Renaissance, a favorite type of composition involved a combination of dances in changing tempos and meters. Some of the dance music developed into stylized pieces for listening, which were not intended for actual dancing. *Terpsichore,* by German composer Michael Praetorius, is a collection of 312 short dance pieces, written in four, five or six parts, with no particular instrumentation specified.

You will hear authentic early instruments in this recording. By listening carefully, guess which modern-day instruments are descended from these early ones.

Check Your Understanding

1. List three major nonmusical changes that took place during the Renaissance period.
2. Describe polyphony as heard in "As Vesta Was Descending."
3. Describe how music from the Renaissance is different from music of today.

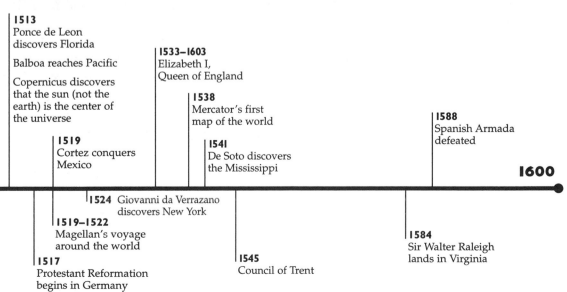

1513
Ponce de Leon
discovers Florida

Balboa reaches Pacific

Copernicus discovers
that the sun (not the
earth) is the center of
the universe

1519
Cortez conquers
Mexico

1533–1603
Elizabeth I,
Queen of England

1538
Mercator's first
map of the world

1541
De Soto discovers
the Mississippi

1588
Spanish Armada
defeated

1600

1524 Giovanni da Verrazano
discovers New York

1519–1522
Magellan's voyage
around the world

1517
Protestant Reformation
begins in Germany

1545
Council of Trent

1584
Sir Walter Raleigh
lands in Virginia

MUSIC&ART

The work of the Italian painter Orazio Gentileschi (1563–1639) was influenced by the innovative style of Caravaggio. In later years, Orazio's works tend to place a single figure or a restricted figure group in sharp relief before a dark background. The subject of this painting, St. Cecilia, is often referred to as the patron saint of music. She is playing a small table pipe organ.

Orazio Gentileschi. *Saint Cecilia and an Angel.* c. 1610. Oil on canvas. 87.8 x 108.1 cm (34 5/8 x 42 1/2"). National Gallery of Art, Washington, D. C. Samuel H. Kress Collection.

Focus

- Describe the Baroque period, including important developments.
- Describe characteristics of Baroque music.

The Baroque Period— A Time of Elaboration

The **Baroque period** *(1600–1750)* was a time of powerful kings and their courts. In Europe, elaborate clothing, hats and hairstyles for the wealthy men and women matched the decorated buildings, gardens, furniture and paintings of this period. The term *baroque* comes from a French word for "imperfect or irregular pearls." Often, pearls were used as decorations on clothing.

There was a great interest in science and exploration. During the Baroque period, Galileo perfected the telescope by 1610, providing the means for greater exploration of the universe. Sir Isaac Newton identified gravity and formulated principles of physics and mathematics. Bartolomeo Cristofori developed the modern pianoforte in which hammers strike the strings. Exploration of new worlds continued, and colonization of places discovered during the Renaissance increased.

Most paintings and sculptures of the time were characterized by their large scale and dramatic details. Artwork celebrated the splendor of royal rulers. For example, the Palace at Versailles near Paris, was built and decorated as a magnificent setting for King Louis XIV of France. It features notably elaborate architecture, paintings, sculptures and gardens.

The Baroque period was a time of great changes brought about through the work of extraordinary people such as:

- Johann Sebastian Bach—German composer
- Orazio Gentileschi—Italian painter
- Alexander Pope—English poet
- Galileo Galilei—Italian mathematician who used his new telescope to prove that the Milky Way is made up of individual stars

COMPOSERS

Johann Pachelbel
(1653–1706)

Antonio Vivaldi
(1678–1741)

Johann Sebastian Bach
(1685–1750)

George Frideric Handel
(1685–1759)

ARTISTS

El Greco
(1541–1614)

Orazio Gentileschi
(1563–1639)

Peter Paul Rubens
(1577–1640)

Rembrandt van Rijn
(1606–1669)

Jan Steen
(1626–1679)

Jan Vermeer
(1632–1675)

AUTHORS

Ben Jonson
(1572–1637)

René Descartes
(1596–1650)

John Milton
(1608–1674)

Molière
(1622–1673)

Alexander Pope
(1688–1744)

Samuel Johnson
(1709–1784)

VOCABULARY

Baroque period

basso continuo

opera

oratorio

concerto grosso

Baroque Music

The music of the Baroque period shows the same kind of dramatic flair that characterized the clothing, architecture and art of the time. Most of the compositions of that period have a strong sense of movement, often including a **basso continuo**, or *a continually moving bass line*.

The Baroque period brought about a great interest in instrumental music. Keyboard instruments were refined, including the clavichord, harpsichord and organ. The modern string family of instruments were now used, and the trumpet became a favorite melody instrument in orchestras.

During the Baroque period, a number of new forms of music were developed. **Opera**, *a combination of singing, instrumental music, dancing and drama that tells a story*, was created beginning with *Orfeo*, by Claudio Monteverdi (1567–1643). The **oratorio**, *a large-scale work for solo voices, chorus and orchestra based on a literary or religious theme*, was also developed. In 1741, George Frideric Handel (1685–1759) composed the *Messiah*, one of the most famous oratorios still performed today. The **concerto grosso** *(a multi-movement Baroque piece for a group of soloists and an orchestra)* was also made popular with Antonio Vivaldi's (1678–1741) *The Four Seasons* and Johann Sebastian Bach's (1685–1750) *Brandenberg Concertos*.

Performance Links

When performing music of the Baroque period, it is important to apply the following guidelines:

- Sing with accurate pitch.
- Be conscious of who has the dominant theme and make sure the accompanying part or parts do not overshadow the melody.
- Keep a steady, unrelenting pulse in most pieces. Precision of dotted rhythms is especially important.
- When dynamic level changes occur, all vocal lines need to change together.

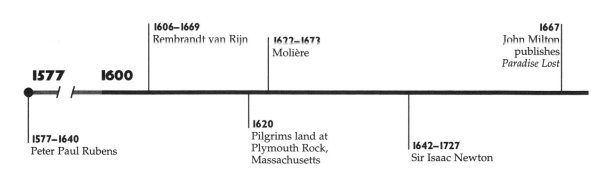

1577   1600

1606–1669
Rembrandt van Rijn

1622–1673
Molière

1667
John Milton
publishes
Paradise Lost

1577–1640
Peter Paul Rubens

1620
Pilgrims land at
Plymouth Rock,
Massachusetts

1642–1727
Sir Isaac Newton

Listening Links

CHORAL SELECTION

"Gloria in excelsis Deo" from *Gloria in D Major* by Antonio Vivaldi (1678–1741)

Antonio Vivaldi was one of the greatest composers and violinists of his time. He wrote operas and concertos, as well as sacred works (oratorios, motets and masses) for chorus, soloists and orchestra. One of his most popular choral works is the *Gloria in D Major* mass. "Gloria in excelsis Deo" is a magnificent choral piece. It is full of energy and emotion that is expressed with great drama. It was composed for three solo voices and chorus, and is accompanied by a variety of instruments. Does ornamentation occur in the vocal parts, in the accompaniment, or both?

INSTRUMENTAL SELECTION

"The Arrival of the Queen of Sheba" from *Solomon* by George Frideric Handel (1685–1759)

George Frideric Handel was a German-born composer who lived in England for most of his life. The oratorio *Solomon* tells the story of King Solomon, of tenth-century Israel. Solomon was known for his great wisdom. Sheba, the Queen of Ethiopia, came to visit and challenge Solomon, but he wisely answered all her questions, and she left as an ally. *Solomon* was written for two choruses, five soloists, a chamber orchestra and a harpsichord. Two instruments are featured playing a duet in this piece. What is the name of these instruments, and to what instrument family do they belong?

Check Your Understanding

1. List three major nonmusical developments that took place during the Baroque period.

2. How would the performance of the oratorio *Solomon* differ from the performance of an opera?

3. Describe how music from the Baroque period is different from music of the Renaissance.

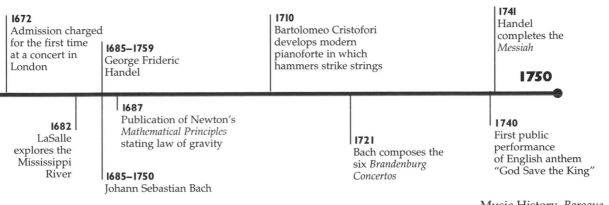

1672
Admission charged for the first time at a concert in London

1685–1759
George Frideric Handel

1710
Bartolomeo Cristofori develops modern pianoforte in which hammers strike strings

1741
Handel completes the *Messiah*

1750

1682
LaSalle explores the Mississippi River

1687
Publication of Newton's *Mathematical Principles* stating law of gravity

1685–1750
Johann Sebastian Bach

1721
Bach composes the six *Brandenburg Concertos*

1740
First public performance of English anthem "God Save the King"

French artist Elisabeth Vigée-LeBrun (1755–1842) lived and worked in Paris during the time of the French Revolution and was forced to flee the city in disguise in 1789. A majority of Vigeé-LeBrun paintings are portraits of women and children. This painting expresses friendship and maternal love.

Elisabeth Vigée-LeBrun. *The Marquise de Pezé and the Marquise de Rouget with Her Two Children.* 1787. Oil on canvas. 123.4 x 155.9 cm (48 5/8 x 61 3/8"). National Gallery of Art, Washington, D. C. Gift of the Bay Foundation in memory of Josephine Bay and Ambassador Charles Ulrick Bay.

Focus

- Describe the Classical period, including important developments.
- Describe characteristics of Classical music.

The Classical Period— A Time of Balance, Clarity and Simplicity

The **Classical period** *(1750–1820)* was a time when people became influenced by the early Greeks and Romans for examples of order and ways of living life. Travelers of the period visited the ruins of ancient Egypt, Rome and Greece and brought the ideas of the ancients to the art and architecture of the time. As a result, the calm beauty and simplicity of this classical art from the past inspired artists and musicians to move away from the overly decorated styles of the Baroque period. The music, art and architecture reflected a new emphasis on emotional restraint and simplicity.

In the intellectual world, there was increasing emphasis on individual reason and enlightenment. Writers such as Voltaire and Thomas Jefferson suggested that through science and democracy, rather than mystery and monarchy, people could choose their own fate. Such thinking, brought on by the enlarging middle class and the excesses of the wealthy royal class, was the beginning of important political changes in society. In many parts of Europe, the power and authority of royalty were attacked, and members of the middle class struggled for their rights. There was a revolution against England by the American colonies, which resulted in the establishment of the United States. In France, the monarchy was overthrown, and the king and most of his court were beheaded.

Some of the most important contributors of the time were:

- Wolfgang Amadeus Mozart—Austrian composer
- Elisabeth Vigée-Lebrun—French painter
- Ben Franklin—American writer, inventor, diplomat
- Joseph Priestley—English chemist who discovered oxygen
- Robert Fulton—American inventor who produced the first submarine, "Nautilus"

COMPOSERS

Carl Philipp Emanuel Bach
(1714–1788)

Johann Christian Bach
(1735–1762)

Franz Joseph Haydn
(1732–1809)

Wolfgang Amadeus Mozart
(1756–1791)

Ludwig van Beethoven
(1770–1827)

ARTISTS

Louis de Carmontelle
(1717–1806)

Thomas Gainsborough
(1727–1788)

Francisco Göya
(1746–1828)

Jacques-Louis David
(1748–1825)

Elisabeth Vigée-Lebrun
(1755–1842)

AUTHORS

Voltaire
(1694–1778)

Benjamin Franklin
(1706–1790)

William Wordsworth
(1770–1850)

Jane Austen
(1775–1817)

VOCABULARY

Classical period

chamber music

symphony

crescendo

decrescendo

sonata-allegro form

Music of the Classical Period

The music of the Classical period was based on balance, clarity and simplicity. Like the architecture of ancient Greece, music was fit together in "building blocks" by balancing one four-bar phrase against another. Classical music was more restrained than the music of the Baroque period, when flamboyant embellishments were common.

The piano replaced the harpsichord and became a favorite instrument of composers. Many concertos were written for the piano. The string quartet was a popular form of **chamber music** (*music performed by a small instrumental ensemble, generally with one instrument per part*). The **symphony** (*a large-scale work for orchestra*) was also a common type of music during this period. Orchestras continued to develop and expand into four families: brass, percussion, strings and woodwinds. Other forms, such as the opera, mass and oratorio, continued to develop as well.

Two major composers associated with the Classical period are Franz Joseph Haydn (1732–1809) and Wolfgang Amadeus Mozart (1756–1791). A third major composer, Ludwig van Beethoven (1770–1827), began composing during this period. Beethoven's works bridge the gap between the Classical and Romantic periods, and are discussed in the next period.

Performance Links

When performing music of the Classical period, it is important to apply the following guidelines:

- Listen for the melody line so the accompaniment parts do not overshadow it.
- Sing chords in tune.
- Make dynamic level changes that move smoothly through each **crescendo** (*a dynamic marking that indicates to gradually sing or play louder*) and **decrescendo** (*a dynamic marking that indicates to gradually sing or play softer*).
- Keep phrases flowing and connected.

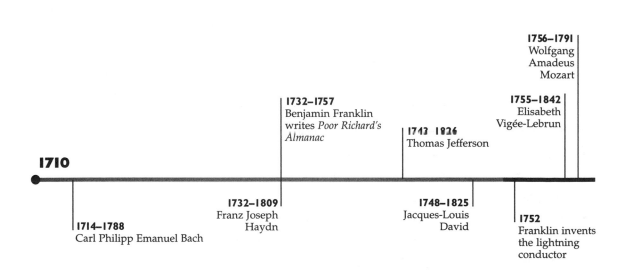

Listening Links

CHORAL SELECTION

"The Heavens Are Telling" from *Creation* by Franz Joseph Haydn (1732–1809)

Franz Joseph Haydn was an Austrian composer who was Beethoven's teacher, and Mozart's friend. The *Creation* is an oratorio based on a poem from John Milton's *Paradise Lost* and the first chapters of the book of Genesis from the Bible. The angels Gabriel, Uriel and Raphael are portrayed by three soloists, and they describe events of each day of the creation. "The Heavens Are Telling" is a grand celebration of praise that alternates between the full chorus and the trio of soloists. List the order of the choral voice parts in the imitative section as they enter with the words, "With wonders of His work."

INSTRUMENTAL SELECTION

Eine Kleine Nachtmusik, First Movement by Wolfgang Amadeus Mozart (1756–1791)

Wolfgang Amadeus Mozart, another Austrian composer, began his musical career at an extremely early age. By the time he was four years old, Mozart had already mastered the keyboard, and by age five, he had written his first composition. Considered one of the greatest composers of all time, he composed 600 musical works.

The first movement of *Eine Kleine Nachtmusik* is written in **sonata-allegro form,** *a large ABA form consisting of three sections: exposition, development and recapitulation.* The Exposition (section A) presents two themes: (a) and (b). Next comes the Development section (section B). The Recapitulation is a return to the original theme (a). Listen to this selection and write down the name for each section of the sonata-allegro form as you hear it.

Check Your Understanding

1. List three major nonmusical changes that took place during the Classical period.

2. Describe the characteristics of Classical music heard in *Eine Kleine Nachtmusik*.

3. Describe how music from the Classical period is different from music of the Baroque period.

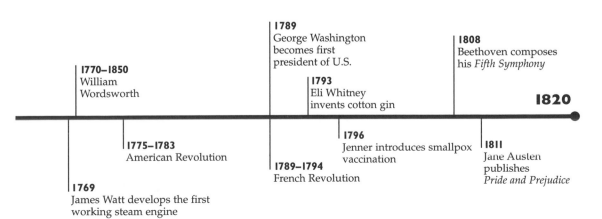

1770–1850
William Wordsworth

1789
George Washington becomes first president of U.S.

1808
Beethoven composes his *Fifth Symphony*

1793
Eli Whitney invents cotton gin

1820

1775–1783
American Revolution

1796
Jenner introduces smallpox vaccination

1811
Jane Austen publishes *Pride and Prejudice*

1789–1794
French Revolution

1769
James Watt develops the first working steam engine

 The American artist George Caleb Bingham (1811–1879) was born in Virginia and raised in Missouri. He became known for his river scenes, often of boatmen bringing cargo to the American West along the Missouri and Mississippi rivers. The scene here is a group of boatmen on a flatboat amusing themselves with their own music and dancing.

George Caleb Bingham. *The Jolly Flatboatmen.* 1846. Oil on canvas. 96.9 x 123.2 cm (38 1/8 x 48 1/2"). National Gallery of Art, Washington, D. C. Private Collection.

Focus

- Describe the Romantic period, including important developments.
- Describe characteristics of Romantic music.

The Romantic Period— A Time of Drama

A new sense of political and artistic freedom emerged during the **Romantic period** *(1820–1900)*. The period began in the middle of the Industrial Revolution, a time when manufacturing became mechanized and many people left farm life to work and live in cities where the manufacturing plants were located. Scientific and mechanical achievements were made in the development of railroads, steamboats, the telegraph and telephone, photography, and sound recordings.

The Industrial Revolution caused a major change in the economic and social life of the common people and also produced a wealthy middle class. More people were able to take part in cultural activities, such as attending music performances and going to art museums. Musicians and artists experienced greater freedom to express their individual creative ideas. This was because they were able to support themselves by ticket sales or sales of their art, instead of relying on the patronage of royalty or the church.

As people moved into the cities, nature and life in the country became the inspiration for many artists. The paintings of William Turner expressed the feelings suggested by nature. Later, French Impressionistic painters, including Claude Monet and Pierre-Auguste Renoir, developed new techniques bringing nature and natural light alive for the viewer.

Some of the most prominent thinkers and creators of this period were:

- Georges Bizet—French composer
- George Caleb Bingham—American painter
- Charles Dickens—English author
- Samuel F. B. Morse—American inventor who developed the telegraph

COMPOSERS

Ludwig van Beethoven (1770–1827)

Franz Schubert (1797–1828)

Felix Mendelssohn (1809–1847)

Frédéric Chopin (1810–1849)

Franz Liszt (1811–1886)

Richard Wagner (1813–1883)

Giuseppe Verdi (1813–1901)

Bedrich Smetana (1824–1884)

Johannes Brahms (1833–1897)

Georges Bizet (1838–1875)

Peter Ilyich Tchaikovsky (1840–1893)

Antonín Dvořák (1841–1904)

Claude Debussy (1862–1918)

ARTISTS

George Caleb Bingham (1811–1879)

Edgar Degas (1834–1917)

Paul Cezanne (1839–1906)

Auguste Rodin (1840–1917)

Claude Monet (1840–1926)

Pierre-Auguste Renoir (1841–1919)

Mary Cassatt (1845–1926)

Paul Gauguin (1848–1903)

Vincent van Gogh (1853–1890)

AUTHORS

Alexandre Dumas (1802–1870)

Henry Wadsworth Longfellow (1807–1882)

Charles Dickens (1812–1870)

Jules Verne (1828–1905)

Louisa May Alcott (1832–1884)

Mark Twain (1835–1910)

Rudyard Kipling (1865–1905)

VOCABULARY

Romantic period

music critic

overture

symphonic poem

Music of the Romantic Period

Music of the Romantic period focused on both the heights and depths of human emotion. The new musical ideas were expressed through larger works with complex vocal melodies and colorful harmonies. During this time, most of the brass and woodwind instruments developed into what they are today, and these instruments were used to add more tone and depth to the music.

Composers began to think about selling their music to the new audiences of middle-class people. Two types of music that appealed to these audiences were the extravagant spectacles of opera and the boldness of grand symphonic music. As music became public, it became subject to public scrutiny, particularly by music critics. A **music critic** is *a writer who gives an evaluation of a musical performance.*

Much of the music of the time was related to literature, such as Felix Mendelssohn's (1809–1847) *A Midsummer Night's Dream*, which was based on the play by William Shakespeare. A well-known section of this work is the **overture**, or *a piece for orchestra that serves as an introduction to an opera or other dramatic work.* The **symphonic poem** is *a single-movement work for orchestra, inspired by a painting, play or other literary or visual work.* Franz Liszt (1811–1886) was a prominent composer of this style of music. The Romantic period was also a time of nationalism, which was reflected in works such as Liszt's *Hungarian Dances*, Richard Wagner's focus on Germanic music, and the tributes to Italy found in Giuseppe Verdi's operas.

Performance Links

When performing music of the Romantic period, it is important to apply the following guidelines:

- Understand the relation of the text to the melody and harmony.
- Concentrate on phrasing, and maintain a clear, beautiful melodic line.
- Perform accurately the wide range of dynamics and tempos.
- Sing confidently in foreign languages to reflect nationalism in music.

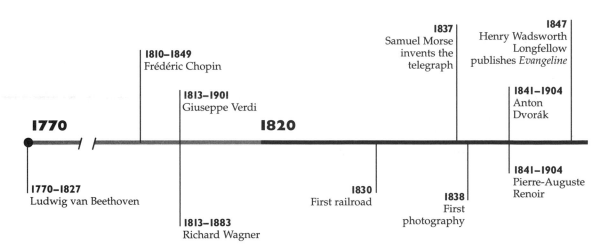

1837
Samuel Morse invents the telegraph

1847
Henry Wadsworth Longfellow publishes *Evangeline*

1810–1849
Frédéric Chopin

1813–1901
Giuseppe Verdi

1841–1904
Anton Dvorák

1770

1820

1770–1827
Ludwig van Beethoven

1830
First railroad

1838
First photography

1841–1904
Pierre-Auguste Renoir

1813–1883
Richard Wagner

Listening Links

CHORAL SELECTION

"Toreador Chorus" from *Carmen* by Georges Bizet (1838–1875)

Carmen, by French composer Georges Bizet, is considered to be one of the most popular operas ever written. The opera tells the story of a gypsy girl who is arrested when she gets into a fight. Placed in the custody of the soldier Don Jose, Carmen soon entices him into a love affair. She then meets Escamilio, a toreador (bullfighter), and tries to get rid of Don Jose. Jilted, Don Jose stabs Carmen and kills himself. The "Toreador Chorus" is heard during the Procession of the Bullfighters. As you listen to the music, write two or three sentences to describe this procession scene in the opera as you think it would look.

INSTRUMENTAL SELECTION

"The Moldau" by Bedrich Smetana (1824–1884)

Bedrich Smetana was a prominent Czech composer. Smetana had a passion for music and composed in spite of his father's desire for him to become a lawyer. His musical efforts were focused mainly on trying to produce Czech national music based on the folk songs and dances that already existed. Smetana awoke one morning to find himself totally deaf. This created a depression that stayed with him through the remainder of his life. "The Moldau" represents Smetana's deep feeling about the beauty and significance of the river that flows through the city of Prague.

Check Your Understanding

1. List three major nonmusical changes that took place during the Romantic period.

2. Describe how "The Moldau" reflects nationalism in music of the Romantic period.

3. Describe how music of the Romantic period is different from music of another period.

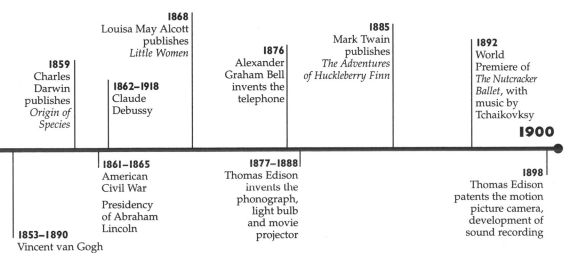

1859 Charles Darwin publishes *Origin of Species*

1868 Louisa May Alcott publishes *Little Women*

1862–1918 Claude Debussy

1876 Alexander Graham Bell invents the telephone

1885 Mark Twain publishes *The Adventures of Huckleberry Finn*

1892 World Premiere of *The Nutcracker Ballet*, with music by Tchaikovksy

1900

1861–1865 American Civil War

Presidency of Abraham Lincoln

1877–1888 Thomas Edison invents the phonograph, light bulb and movie projector

1898 Thomas Edison patents the motion picture camera, development of sound recording

1853–1890 Vincent van Gogh

 **MUSIC & ART**

African American artist Romare Howard Bearden (1911–1988) is recognized as one of the most creative visual artists of the twentieth century. He experimented with many different styles and mediums but found a unique form of expression in collage. He had a great interest in literature, history, music, mathematics and the performing arts.

Romare Bearden. *The Piano Lesson (Homage to Mary Lou)*. 1983. Color lithograph on paper. 75.2 x 52.3 cm (29 1/2 x 20 1/2"). The Pennsylvania Academy of the Fine Arts, Philadelphia, Pennsylvania. The Harold A. and Ann R. Sorgenti Collection of Contemporary African American Art.

Focus

- Describe the Contemporary period, including important developments.
- Describe characteristics of Contemporary music.

The Contemporary Period— The Search for Originality

Nothing characterizes the **Contemporary period** *(1900–present)* better than technology. Many technological advances began on October 4, 1957, when the Soviet Union successfully launched *Sputnik I*, the world's first artificial satellite. While the Sputnik launch was a single event, it marked the start of the Space Age and began many new political, military, technological and scientific developments.

Isolation was greatly reduced worldwide by developments in travel (rail, sea and air) and communication (telephone, radio, television and the Internet). It was also reduced as countries came together during World War I and World War II. Elements of cultures merged as people moved from their countries to various parts of the world for economic, political or social reasons. It no longer seems strange, for example, to see Chinese or Mexican restaurants in most communities in the United States or McDonald's® restaurants in Europe and Asia.

Some of the noteworthy leaders of this period have been:

- Igor Stravinsky—Russian/American composer
- Romare Bearden—American artist
- Robert Frost—American poet
- Wilbur and Orville Wright—American inventors who designed and flew the first airplane
- Albert Einstein—German/American scientist who formulated theories of relativity

COMPOSERS

Sergei Rachmaninoff (1873–1943)
Arnold Schoenberg (1874–1951)
Béla Bartók (1881–1945)
Igor Stravinsky (1882–1971)
Sergey Prokofiev (1891–1953)
Carl Orff (1895–1982)
Aaron Copland (1900–1990)
Benjamin Britten (1913–1976)
Leonard Bernstein (1918–1990)
Moses Hogan (1957–2003)

ARTISTS

Henri Matisse (1869–1954)
Pablo Picasso (1881–1973)
Wassily Kandinsky (1866–1944)
Marc Chagall (1887–1985)
Georgia O'Keeffe (1887–1986)
Romare Howard Bearden (1911–1988)
Andy Warhol (1930–1987)

AUTHORS

Robert Frost (1874–1963)
Virginia Woolf (1882–1941)
Ernest Hemingway (1899–1961)
Rachel Carson (1907–1964)
James Baldwin (1924–1997)
JK Rowling (b. 1965)

VOCABULARY

Contemporary period
synthesizer
twelve-tone music
aleatory music
fusion

Music of the Contemporary Period

Technology has had a large influence on Contemporary music. Most people have access to music via radio, television and recordings. Technology has also influenced the music itself. The invention of electrified and electronic instruments led many composers to experiment with the new sounds. One of the most important new instruments was the **synthesizer**, *a musical instrument that produces sounds electronically, rather than by the physical vibrations of an acoustic instrument.*

The Contemporary period has witnessed a number of musical styles. Maurice Ravel (1875–1937) and Claude Debussy (1862–1918), for example, wrote music in the Impressionist style, often describing an impression of nature. Some of the music of Igor Stravinsky (1882–1971) and others was written in a neo-Classical (or "new" classical) style. Other music was considered avant-garde (or unorthodox or experimental); this included Arnold Schoenberg's (1874–1951) **twelve-tone music**, *a type of music that uses all twelve tones of the scale equally.* Composers experimented with **aleatory music**, or *a type of music in which certain aspects are performed randomly and left to chance.*

In addition, composers began using the rhythms, melodies and texts of other cultures in their compositions in a trend called **fusion**, or *the act of combining various types and cultural influences of music into a new style.*

Performance Links

When performing music of the Contemporary period, it is important to apply the following guidelines:

- Sing on pitch, even in extreme parts of your range.
- Tune intervals carefully in the skips found in many melodic lines.
- Sing changing meters and unusual rhythm patterns precisely.
- Perform accurately the wide range of dynamics and tempos.

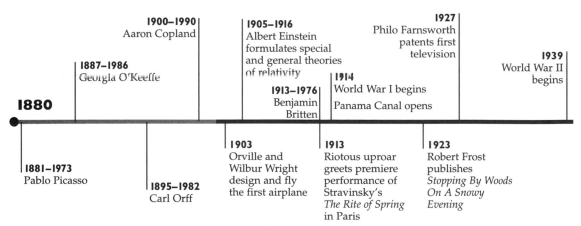

1900–1990
Aaron Copland

1887–1986
Georgia O'Keeffe

1905–1916
Albert Einstein formulates special and general theories of relativity

1927
Philo Farnsworth patents first television

1939
World War II begins

1913–1976
Benjamin Britten

1914
World War I begins
Panama Canal opens

1880

1881–1973
Pablo Picasso

1895–1982
Carl Orff

1903
Orville and Wilbur Wright design and fly the first airplane

1913
Riotous uproar greets premiere performance of Stravinsky's *The Rite of Spring* in Paris

1923
Robert Frost publishes *Stopping By Woods On A Snowy Evening*

Listening Links

CHORAL SELECTION

"The Battle of Jericho," Traditional Spiritual, arranged by Moses George Hogan (1957–2003)

Moses Hogan, born in New Orleans, Louisiana, was a pianist, conductor and arranger. He has been one of the most influential arrangers of our time in the revitalization of the songs of our forebearers. His contemporary settings of African American spirituals have been revered by audiences and praised by critics. He had a unique talent for expanding the harmonies and rhythms while preserving the traditional essence of these spirituals. Hogan's arrangements have become staples in the repertoires of choirs worldwide. What specific musical effects did Hogan add in his arrangement of "The Battle of Jericho"?

INSTRUMENTAL SELECTION

"Infernal Dance of King Kaschei" from *The Firebird* by Igor Stravinsky (1882–1971)

Igor Stravinsky was born in Russia, but lived the last twenty-five years of his life in California. *The Firebird* is a ballet that begins when Prince Ivan gives a magical golden bird with wings of fire its freedom in return for a feather. With the help of the magic feather, Ivan conquers an evil king and frees the princesses and prisoners that the king had held captive. Prince Ivan falls in love with a princess and they live happily ever after.

In the first section of this piece, you can hear the loud shrieks of the firebird. How many times did you hear this sudden loud sound?

Check Your Understanding

1. List three major nonmusical changes that took place during the Contemporary period.

2. Discuss the differences between a composer and an arranger.

3. Describe how music of the Contemporary period is different from music of the Romantic period.

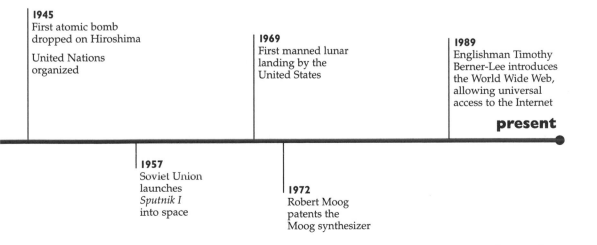

1945
First atomic bomb
dropped on Hiroshima

United Nations
organized

1957
Soviet Union
launches
Sputnik I
into space

1969
First manned lunar
landing by the
United States

1972
Robert Moog
patents the
Moog synthesizer

1989
Englishman Timothy
Berner-Lee introduces
the World Wide Web,
allowing universal
access to the Internet

present

SPOTLIGHT

Careers In Music

Teacher

Music teachers share their love of music with their students. To become a public school teacher, you must have a bachelor's degree in music education. That will require at least four years of college, including one semester of student teaching. High school and junior high music teachers usually specialize in one performance area such as choir, band or orchestra. They may also teach general music, music theory, music appreciation, keyboard and guitar. Elementary music teachers enjoy working with young children. Their job is varied in that they teach singing, dancing, how to play instruments, listening, world music and much more.

At the college level, a music professor must have additional training. Although the minimum requirement is to have a master's degree in music, most colleges require you to have a doctorate as well. College professors teach students how to become professional musicians and professional teachers.

Some musicians choose to teach music through their church or synagogue. Church musicians may be full-time or part-time employees. They might serve as a singer, a choir director, an organist, an instrumentalist or a **cantor** (*a person who sings and teaches music in temples or synagogues*). Some of these positions require a college degree in music.

Private studio teachers enjoy working with students on a one-on-one basis. They teach from their homes, from a private studio, or sometimes at a school. Private instructors teach voice, piano/keyboard, or any of the musical instruments. Their hours are flexible, but they often work in the evenings or weekends because that is when their students are not in school.

Choral Library

¡Aleluya, Amén! 130

Bound For The Rio Grande 136

City Called Heaven 148

Duond Akuru 156

I Know Where I'm Goin' 168

Kyrie 178

Lakota Wiyanki 186

Miserere Nobis 194

The River Sleeps Beneath The Sky 204

Set Me As A Seal 212

Sing Out This Maytime 216

The Wells Fargo Wagon 227

¡Aleluya, Amén!

Composer: Rafael D. Grullón
Text: Traditional Liturgy
Voicing: SATB

VOCABULARY

mangulina

mixed meter

Focus

- Perform music in mixed meter.
- Perform music representing the Dominican Republic culture.

Getting Started

What do these words have in common?

> ...*Santa Domingo*
>
> ...*sugar cane*
>
> ...*merengue*

 **SKILL BUILDERS**

To learn more about mixed meter, see Intermediate Sight-Singing, *page 97.*

They describe three important aspects of the Dominican Republic. Santa Domingo is the capital city, sugar cane is the major agricultural crop, and the merengue is the most famous traditional dance from this Caribbean country that shares the island of Hispaniola with Haiti.

◆ History and Culture

The Dominican Republic is also known for its dynamic union of three great cultures: African, European and the indigenous culture of the island. This vibrant blend of traditions is most apparent in the food, music and religious beliefs of the population. "¡Aleluya, Amén!" could also be considered a cultural mix. Composer Rafael Grullón (b. 1933) chose a Spanish sacred text and set it to the captivating rhythms of the **mangulina,** another *traditional dance from the Dominican Republic.* This dance developed from the merging of African and European dance steps and rhythms. "¡Aleluya, Amén!" is written in **mixed meter,** or *a technique in which the time signature changes frequently within a piece.* In this song, every measure alternates between $\frac{6}{8}$ and $\frac{3}{4}$ meters. All these elements combine to make "¡Aleluya, Amén!" a song of joyful celebration—just what you would expect to hear on a beautiful tropical island.

Links to Learning

◆ Vocal

Read and perform the following melodic pattern that outlines the G minor scale. A **minor scale** is *a scale that has* la *as its keynote or home tone.*

la ti do re mi re do ti la si la

la ti do re mi re do ti la si la

◆ Theory

To alternate between $\frac{6}{8}$ meter and $\frac{3}{4}$ meter, it is necessary to keep the eighth note constant. Although there are 6 eighth notes in both meters, in $\frac{6}{8}$ meter, the dotted quarter note receives the beat (3 eighth notes). However, in $\frac{3}{4}$ meter, the quarter note receives the beat (2 eighth notes). Read and perform the following rhythmic pattern by patting your legs with your right and left hands as indicated. Count out loud and stress the numbers 1 and 4 in $\frac{6}{8}$ meter, and the numbers 1, 3 and 5 in $\frac{3}{4}$ meter.

Left hand

Right hand

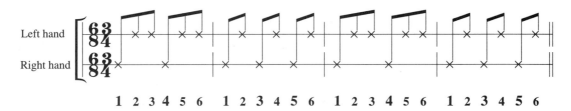

1 2 3 4 5 6   1 2 3 4 5 6   1 2 3 4 5 6   1 2 3 4 5 6

Evaluation

Demonstrate how well you have learned the skills and concepts featured in the lesson "¡Aleluya, Amén!" by completing the following:

- Chant the words in rhythm in measures 9–16, to show your ability to read music in mixed meter.

- Sing "¡Aleluya, Amén!" slowly while clapping the rhythmic pattern described in the Theory section above to feel the changing meter.

¡Aleluya, Amén!

For SATB and Piano with Optional Drums

Words and Music by
RAFAEL D. GRULLÓN

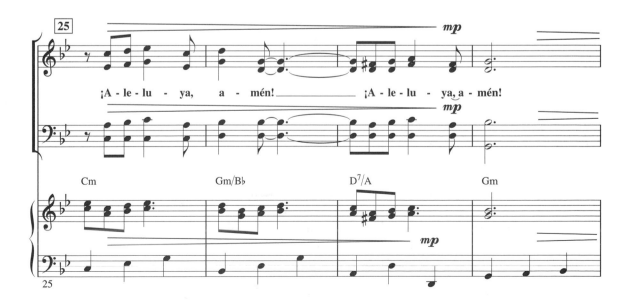

SPOTLIGHT

Changing Voice

As we grow in size and maturity, we don't always grow at the same rate. Just look around your school or neighborhood. Some thirteen-year-olds tower over others, while some are quite small.

As the voice matures, it changes in both pitch and **timbre** *(tone quality)*. Just like growing in stature, this process is not the same for every person. One person's voice might drop an octave almost overnight, while another person's might not seem to have changed at all.

The Male Voice

As a young male singer, you will face several challenges as your voice matures. Certain pitches that were once easy to sing suddenly may be out of your vocal range. While every voice change is unique, many male singers progress through several identifiable stages:

1. The voice is a treble voice with no obvious signs of changing.

2. The upper range sounds slightly breathy or hoarse.

3. The singer is able to sing lower pitches than before. Higher pitches continue to sound breathy. The speaking and singing voices are noticeably lower. There is an obvious "break" around middle C.

4. The voice "settles" into **Bass** *(the lowest-sounding male voice)* or "rises" to **Tenor** *(the highest-sounding male voice)*. Higher pitches can now be sung in **falsetto,** *a register in the male voice that extends far above the natural high voice.*

With practice and attention to the principles of good singing, you can get through this transition without too much difficulty.

The Female Voice

As a young female singer, you will not face the same challenges that young male singers face. However, your voice will go through changes, too.

Between the ages of eleven and sixteen, you might notice breathiness in your vocal tone, difficulty in moving between your chest voice and head voice, and a general lack of vocal resonance.

By using the good vocal techniques of posture, breath and vowel formation, you can establish all the qualities necessary for success. You should use your full vocal range and gain experience in singing both **Alto** *(the lowest-sounding female voice)* and **Soprano** *(the highest-sounding female voice)*, since your actual voice category may not be evident until you reach your middle-to-late teens.

Bound For The Rio Grande

Composer: American Sea Chantey, arranged by Emily Crocker
Text: Traditional
Voicing: 3-Part Mixed

VOCABULARY

sea chantey

compound meter

Focus

- Identify the melody line in music.

- Read and perform music in $\frac{6}{8}$ meter.

- Perform music in the character in which it was written.

 **SPOTLIGHT**

To learn more about changing voice, see page 135.

Getting Started

When it comes to cleaning your room at home, which description best fits you?

1. You love to clean and go right to work.

2. You do not enjoy cleaning, but if you play music or sing, the work gets done.

If you relate to the second statement, you have something in common with eighteenth-century English sailors. "Bound For The Rio Grande" is a **sea chantey,** or *a song sung by sailors in the rhythm of their work.* As they sang, the work was done. You might want to sing this song the next time you clean your room!

◆ History and Culture

More specifically, "Bound For The Rio Grande" is a capstan chantey. The capstan is a mushroom-shaped object on a ship that connects to its anchor. The sailors inserted bars into holes along the top of the capstan. They would turn the capstan to raise the anchor. Capstan chanteys typically have a very steady rhythm and tell long stories because it sometimes took hours to raise the anchor.

Originally, the Rio Grande in this song may have referred to Rio Grande do Sul in Brazil. Ships would leave England and Wales and sail to Brazil for trade. Today, "Bound For The Rio Grande" is considered one of the most popular sea chanteys.

Links to Learning

◆ **Vocal**

The melody to "Bound For The Rio Grande" sometimes takes on the character of the rolling sea. To feel this effect, place an accent on the syllables that fall on the beat as you read and perform the following example.

◆ **Theory**

$\frac{6}{8}$ meter is an example of **compound meter,** or *a meter in which the dotted quarter note receives the beat.* Read and perform the following example with the feel of two beats per measure.

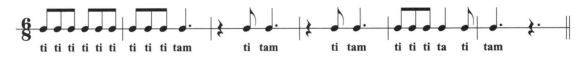

◆ **Artistic Expression**

Pretend you are a sailor pulling a rope with the anchor attached. On the downbeat of each measure, grab the imaginary rope and pull back with resistance. On the second beat of each measure, lift one hand and reach forward as if grabbing the next section of the rope. Continue this two-beat motion as you sing the song.

Evaluation

Demonstrate how well you have learned the skills and concepts featured in the lesson "Bound For The Rio Grande" by completing the following:

- In a small group with at least one person on a part, sing measures 15–20. Raise your hand when your part has the melody. As a group, evaluate how well the melody line could be heard over the other parts.

- Chant the words in rhythm in measures 26–34 to show your ability to read music in $\frac{6}{8}$ meter.

- Stand still and sing measures 7–23 of "Bound For The Rio Grande." Then sing the passage again with the motions described in the Artistic Expression section above. Compare the two performances and decide which one you prefer and why.

Bound For The Rio Grande

For 3-Part Mixed and Piano

Arranged by
EMILY CROCKER

American Sea Chantey

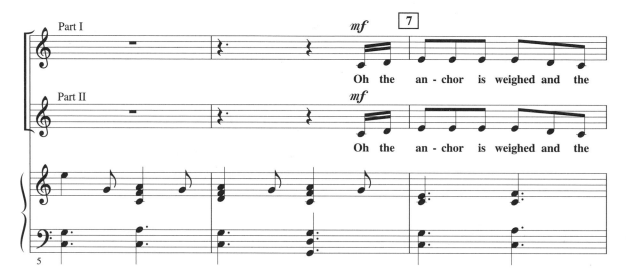

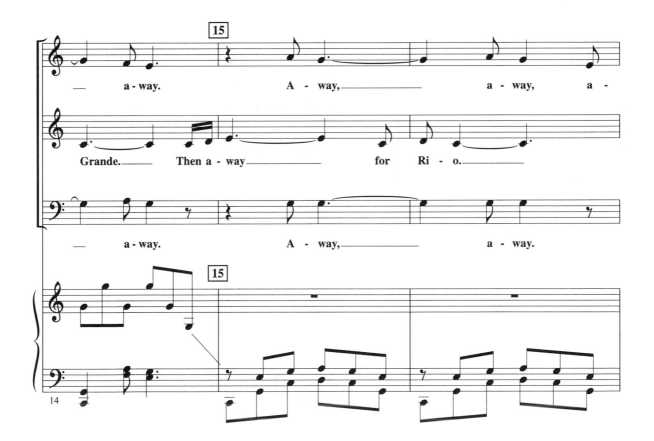

way,_____ for Ri - o._____ Oo._____ We are

A - way,_____ a - way. Oo._____ We are

A - way,_____ a - way. So fare—— ye well,—— my bon - nie young girl.

17

bound for Ri - o,_____ for Ri - o,_____ a - way.

bound for Ri - o, for Ri - o_____ Grande.

We are bound_____ for Ri - o,_____ a - way.

21

Oo. _____ We are bound for Ri - o, _____

Oo. _____ We are bound for Ri - o

jol - ly good mate and a good skip - per too. We are bound, _____

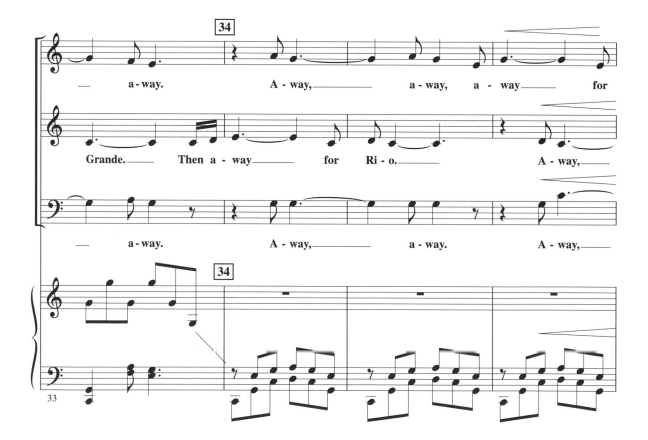

_____ a - way. A - way, _____ a - way, a - way _____ for

Grande. _____ Then a - way _____ for Ri - o. _____ A - way, _____

_____ a - way. A - way, _____ a - way. A - way, _____

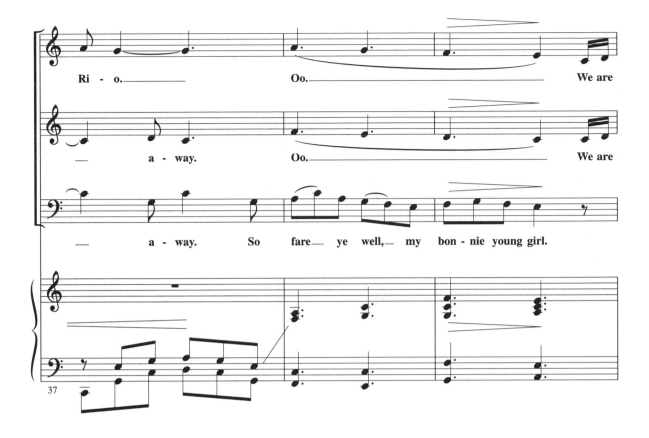

We are bound for Ri - o,_____ Ri - o

We are bound for Ri - o,_____ Ri - o

bon - nie young girl. We are bound for Ri - o,_____ Ri - o

57

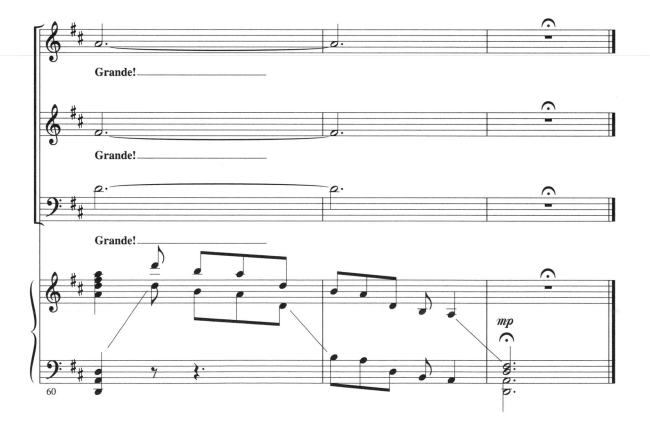

Grande!_____

Grande!_____

Grande!

Grande!_____

60

SPOTLIGHT

Gospel Music

Gospel music is *religious music that originated in the African American churches of the South.* Characteristics of gospel music include improvisation, syncopation and repetition. Following the Civil War, African American churches began to form. The spirituals previously sung by the slaves served as their main source of sacred music. By the early 1900s, some sectors of the church moved to more spirited songs accompanied by tambourines, drums and piano. This new music was the beginning of the gospel style.

African American gospel music gained national recognition during the 1940s and the 1950s with the recordings and live concerts by the singing great Mahalia Jackson (1912–1972). Also of influence was composer and bandleader Thomas Andrew Dorsey (1899–1993). He published over 400 gospel songs and is known as the father of gospel music. His featured music used lively rhythms and syncopated piano accompaniments. "Precious Lord, Take My Hand" is probably his most famous song.

When asked about the correct way to sing gospel music, the contemporary composer Rollo Dilworth said that singers often debate about the appropriate use of chest and head voice registers when performing gospel style. While some believe that excessive use of the chest voice might cause vocal damage, others believe that singing in the African American idiom is not "authentic" if performed in head voice. Dilworth suggests that successful singing in most any genre requires a balanced, healthy singing tone in both head and chest registers. Vocal techniques used in gospel singing include (1) percussive singing (a style that lies between legato and staccato styles); (2) swell (an exaggerated crescendo that adds weight and breadth to an accented syllable); and (3) pitch bending (the scooping up to a pitch, often coupled with a swell or a falling off of a pitch). The rhythm is felt in an accurate yet relaxed style. Basic movements may include stepping, clapping and rocking. Improvisation of the melody is frequently heard in gospel music.

Listen to the recording of "City Called Heaven" (page 148) and identify the characteristics of gospel style singing that you hear.

City Called Heaven

Composer: Traditional Spiritual, arranged by Josephine Poelinitz
Text: Traditional
Voicing: SATB

VOCABULARY

gospel music

improvisation

$\frac{9}{8}$ meter

tenuto

SPOTLIGHT

To learn more about improvisation, see page 177.

Focus

- Read and perform music in $\frac{9}{8}$ meter.
- Identify and perform tenuto markings.
- Perform music that represents the gospel style.

Getting Started

Cultural traditions often pass from elders to children through storytelling. The African American spiritual "City Called Heaven" was probably first sung by slaves. It tells their story of sorrow for life here on Earth and their longing for the freedom and everlasting peace that heaven may bring.

◆ History and Culture

"City Called Heaven" has been arranged by Josephine Poelinitz, who is a choral conductor, arranger and vocal specialist in Chicago, Illinois. She has arranged this particular spiritual in a slow gospel style. **Gospel music** is *religious music that originated in the African American churches of the South and is characterized by improvisation, syncopation and the free extension or repetition of any fragment of the text.* In "City Called Heaven," the choral parts are written in a marked and detached manner consistent with traditional gospel-singing style. Sometimes the full chorus takes the lead, and at other times it performs background material that supports the soloist.

You will enjoy learning the solo line in "City Called Heaven." After you can sing the solo with confidence, try changing the solo by using **improvisation** (*the art of making it up as you sing*).

Links to Learning

◆ **Vocal**

Read and perform the following example to practice chord patterns in the key of F minor found in "City Called Heaven."

◆ **Theory**

"City Called Heaven" is written in $\frac{9}{8}$ **meter,** *a time signature in which there are three groups of eighth notes per measure and the dotted quarter note receives the beat.* The style markings included in this example include **tenuto** (‾◗), *a symbol used to indicate that a note should receive extra stress or be held slightly longer than its given value.* Read and perform the following rhythmic patterns, observing these markings.

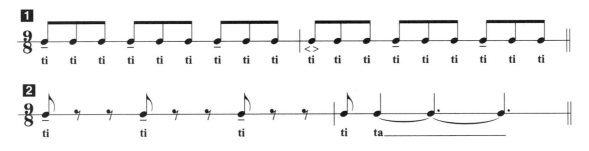

Evaluation

Demonstrate how well you have learned the skills and concepts featured in the lesson "City Called Heaven" by completing the following:

• Record yourself singing measures 5–12. Listen and evaluate how well you were able to perform the rhythms, dynamics and style markings correctly.

• Locate the passages in the music in which the choir has the lead, then locate the passages in which the choir sings background. Discuss how your singing may be different in these two instances.

City Called Heaven

For SATB and Piano

Traditional Spiritual

Arranged by
JOSEPHINE POELINITZ

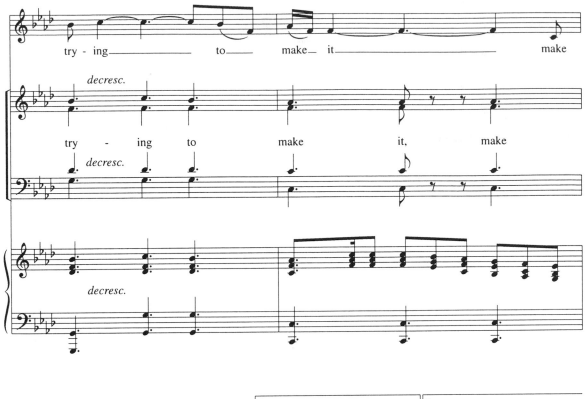

Some-times I'm tossed and I'm driv-en,

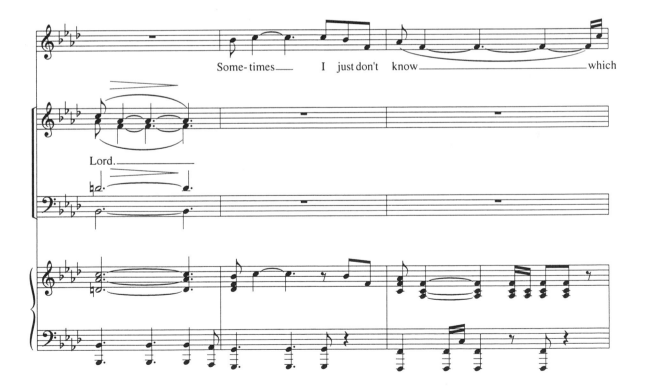

Some-times I just don't know which

Lord.

Duond Akuru

Composer: Rollo A. Dilworth
Text: Rollo A. Dilworth, translation by Theodora Ayot
Voicing: SAB

VOCABULARY

polyrhythms

shekere

Focus

- Read and perform rhythmic patterns that contain syncopation.
- Sing in a foreign language using proper diction (Duoluo).
- Perform music written in the style of African music.

Getting Started

Do you have an inner voice that gives you guidance when you have to make a tough decision, or comfort when you are having a rough day? Do you have a pet or a favorite animal that makes you smile and brings joy to your heart? All over the world, the dove is known as a symbol of peace, joy and love. "Duond Akuru" celebrates the gentle voice, the peaceful character and the natural beauty of this bird.

 **SPOTLIGHT**

To learn more about gospel music, see page 147.

◆ History and Culture

"Duond Akuru" literally means "the dove's voice." This piece was written by Rollo Dilworth in collaboration with Theodora Ayot, a teaching colleague at North Park University in Chicago, Illinois. "Duond Akuru" blends ideas from both African and African American cultures. In addition to English, the Duoluo language, as spoken by the Luo people of Kenya, is used throughout the piece.

Although the African American gospel style serves as a harmonic framework for this piece, "Duond Akuru" also utilizes chant techniques, **polyrhythms** *(several different rhythms performed simultaneously),* and percussion instruments that are inherently African in their origins. To achieve an authentic effect, instruments such as a **shekere** *(an African shaker consisting of a hollow gourd surrounded by beads),* tambourine and congas may be used. Singers are encouraged to perform this piece in a rhythmically jubilant manner.

Links to Learning

◆ **Theory**

Read and perform the following rhythmic patterns found in "Duond Akuru." First clap the rhythms, then add the vowel sounds as indicated.

◆ **Artistic Expression**

To give "Duond Akuru" a more traditional African sound, perform the following rhythmic patterns on percussion instruments (or use body percussion). You may want to add these instruments to your performance.

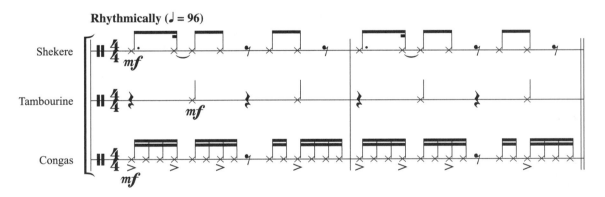

Evaluation

Demonstrate how well you have learned the skills and concepts featured in the lesson "Duond Akuru" by completing the following:

• Chant the words in rhythm to your part in measures 46–54 to show that you can read syncopated rhythms accurately. How did you do?

• Sing measures 46–54 with the Duoluo text. Sing with a smooth transition between the "ah" and "oo" vowels. Evaluate how well you were able to sing with a smooth transition between the vowels.

For the 2003 National ACDA Middle School/Junior High Honors Choir, Henry Leck, Conductor

Duond Akuru
(The Voice of the Dove)

For SAB and Piano with Optional Flute*

Translation by
THEODORA AYOT

Words and Music by
ROLLO A. DILWORTH

*Flute part may be found on page 167.

Duond a - ku - ru. Duond a - ku - ru. Duond a - ku - ru. Duond a - ku - ru.

Soprano
mp
Duond a - ku - ru.

Baritone
Duond a - ku - ru. Duond a - ku - ru. Duond a - ku - ru. Duond a - ku - ru.

Soprano

Alto *mp*
Duond a - ku - ru.

Baritone
Duond a - ku - ru. Duond a - ku - ru. Duond a - ku - ru. Duond a - ku - ru.

*Shekere and tambourine tacet, congas continue ad lib.

high up a-bove,— and it brings laugh-ter and joy to my soul!—
call-ing to me,— and it brings com-fort and love with-out end!

high up a - bove,——— and it brings laugh-ter and joy to my soul!———
call-ing to me,——— and it brings com-fort and love with-out end!———

high up a - bove,——— and it brings laugh-ter and joy to my soul!—
call-ing to me,——— and it brings com-fort and love with-out end!—

(for rehearsal only)

Duond a - ku - ru! E chun-ya a-win - jo wer——— ma-mit.——— A-

*Shekere and tambourine tacet, congas continue ad lib.
**Conga roll ad lib.

Duond Akuru
(The Voice of the Dove)

FLUTE

Words and Music by
ROLLO A. DILWORTH
Translation by
THEODORA AYOT

I Know Where I'm Goin'

Composer: Irish Folk Song, arranged by J. Chris Moore
Text: Traditional
Voicing: 2-Part Mixed

VOCABULARY

folk song

legato

crescendo

decrescendo

phrase

SPOTLIGHT

To learn more about arranging, see page 63.

Focus

- Perform two-part music.
- Sing phrases expressively.
- Perform music representing the Irish culture.

Getting Started

Dorothy

The Scarecrow

The Tin Man

The Cowardly Lion

The characters in "The Wizard of Oz" are focused on their own individual goals. Can you describe each character's goal? Some might call this selfish or stubborn, but others would say that perseverance and focus are virtues.

The young girl in "I Know Where I'm Goin'" is focused on marrying her love, Johnny. In the lyrics, she tells us she would willingly give up many fine things in her life to marry Johnny. However, the conclusion of the story is not clear. After you learn the song, decide whether or not she marries him.

◆ History and Culture

"I Know Where I'm Goin'" is an Irish folk song. **Folk songs** are *songs that have been passed down by word of mouth from generation to generation.* Irish folk music enjoys quite a bit of popularity today and is featured on concerts, stages, radio, television and movies throughout the world. In this arrangement of "I Know Where I'm Goin'," the reflective nature of the text is complemented by an accompaniment in the style of a guitar or other folk instrument. Perhaps your focus can be to remain sensitive to the folk style of the music as you rehearse and perform.

Links to Learning

◆ **Vocal**

Perform the following example to practice singing **legato** (*a style of singing that is connected and sustained*). The **crescendo** (*a dynamic marking that indicates to gradually sing louder*) and **decrescendo** (*a dynamic marking that indicates to gradually sing softer*) add expression and dynamic contrast to your performance.

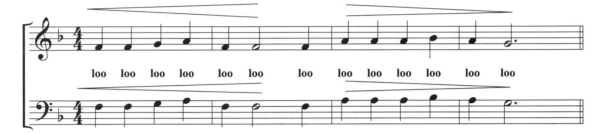

loo   loo   loo   loo   loo   loo   loo   loo   loo   loo   loo   loo   loo

Perform the following example to practice shaping the basic vowel sounds that form the basis for a good choral tone. Sing with the jaw dropped and the corners of your mouth in. Sing in two parts.

hah   hoh   heh   hah   hoo   hee   heh

◆ **Artistic Expression**

A **phrase** is *a musical idea with a beginning and an end*. Sing measures 5–8 in unison while drawing an arch in the air above your head. Shape your phrase by beginning softly, then singing loudest in the middle and soft at the end.

Evaluation

Demonstrate how well you have learned the skills and concepts featured in the lesson "I Know Where I'm Goin'" by completing the following:

• In a duet with one singer on each part, perform measures 25–29. Evaluate how well you were able to sing in two parts.

• Find other phrases in the music. Select one person to come forward and serve as a "phrase leader." Sing each phrase while following the arch shown by the phrase leader. How expressively were you able to sing the phrases?

For Sally

I Know Where I'm Goin'

For 2-Part and Piano

**Arranged by
J. CHRIS MOORE**

Irish Folk Song

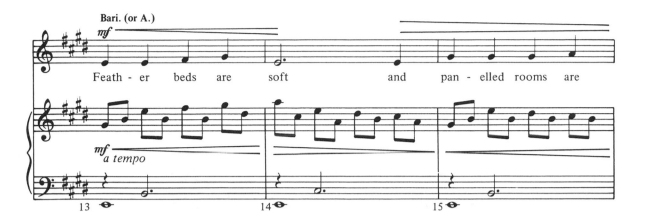

Feath - er beds are soft and pan - elled rooms are

bon - ny, But she would leave them all to___

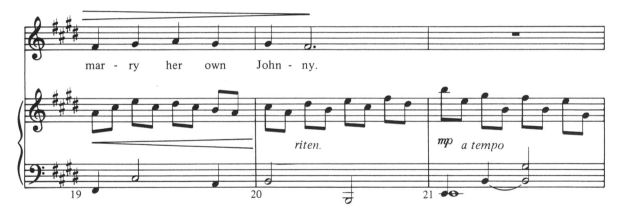

mar - ry her own John - ny.

SPOTLIGHT

Improvisation

Improvisation is *the art of singing or playing music, making it up as you go.* **Scat singing** is *an improvisational style of singing that uses nonsense syllables instead of words.* Sometimes, these nonsense sounds can imitate the sound of an instrument. Scat singing, especially as a solo, can be the scariest part of singing jazz.

Dr. Kirby Shaw, one of the top vocal jazz composers and conductors in the world today, offers the following suggestions to help build your confidence in this fun and exciting art form.

Start your scat solo with a short melodic or rhythmic idea from the tune being performed. There is nothing wrong in having a preconceived idea before starting to sing a scat solo! By gradually developing the idea as you sing, you will have an organized solo that sounds completely improvised.

Start with scat syllables like "doo" when singing swing tunes. Try "bee," "dee," and "dn" for occasional accented eighth notes on the *and* of beats (1 *and* 2 *and* 3 *and* 4 *and*). Try "doot" or "dit" for short last notes of a musical phrase.

Be able to imitate any sound you like from the world around you, such as a soft breeze, a car horn or a musical instrument. There might be a place for that sound in one of your solos.

Listen to and imitate, note-for-note, the great jazz singers or instrumentalists. You can be inspired by musicians like Ella Fitzgerald, Jon Hendricks, Louis Armstrong or Charlie Parker.

Learn to sing the blues. You can listen to artists like B. B. King, Stevie Ray Vaughan, Buddy Guy or Luther Allison. There are many types of recordings from which to choose.

In short, learn as many different kinds of songs as you can. The best scat singers quote from such diverse sources as nursery rhymes, African chant and even opera. Above all, have fun as you develop your skills!

Kyrie

Composer: Andrea Klouse
Text: Liturgical Latin
Voicing: SAB

 SPOTLIGHT

*To learn more about
pitch matching,
see page 77.*

Focus

- Perform music with accurate pitch matching.

- Identify ABA form and coda.

- Perform music that represents the Contemporary period.

Getting Started

One interesting benefit of singing in a choir is that you learn songs in foreign languages. Make a list of all the foreign-language choir songs you know. How many languages are on your list? Do you know songs in Spanish, French, German, Hebrew or Latin? When you learn a song in the original language, you can understand how the composer actually wanted the words to fit the music.

◆ History and Culture

The "Kyrie" is one of the principal sections in the **mass,** *a religious service of prayers and ceremonies.* Although the traditional language of the mass is Latin, the word *Kyrie* is actually a Greek word that was adapted into the Latin mass. Composers throughout the centuries have set the words of the "Kyrie" to music. Because there are only three lines of text—

> *Kyrie eleison* (Lord have mercy)
>
> *Christie eleison* (Christ have mercy)
>
> *Kyrie eleison* (Lord have mercy)

—"Kyrie" composers often use ABA form for the music. **ABA form** is *the design in which the opening phrases (section A) are followed by contrasting phrases (section B), which leads to a repetition of the opening phrases (section A).* Composer Andrea Klouse has also added a **coda,** or *a special ending to a song,* to her "Kyrie." Find these sections in the music. After you learn "Kyrie," you can add another foreign-language song to your list!

Links to Learning

◆ **Vocal**

Accurate **pitch matching** *(singing on the same pitch as those around you)* requires that you hear the note in your head before you sing. Perform the following example to practice singing on pitch. Avoid unwanted scoops and slides in the vocal line.

◆ **Theory**

The A sections in "Kyrie" are based on the A minor scale. A **minor scale** is *a scale in which* la *is the keynote or home tone.* Sing the A minor scale below.

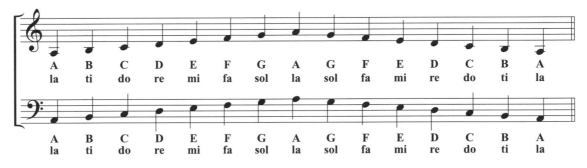

Evaluation

Demonstrate how well you have learned the skills and concepts featured in the lesson "Kyrie" by completing the following:

- Sing measures 13–21 for a classmate. Evaluate how well you were able to sing the pitches in tune without scooping or sliding.

- Describe the form of "Kyrie." Identify the measure numbers that mark the beginning of each section (ABA) and the coda. Compare your choices with those of a classmate. How did you do?

Kyrie

For SAB and Piano

Liturgical Latin

Music by
ANDREA KLOUSE

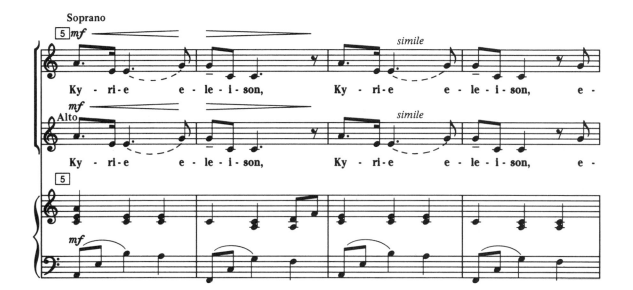

*Accent the "k" in "Kyrie" gently to ensure a clean "echo" effect.

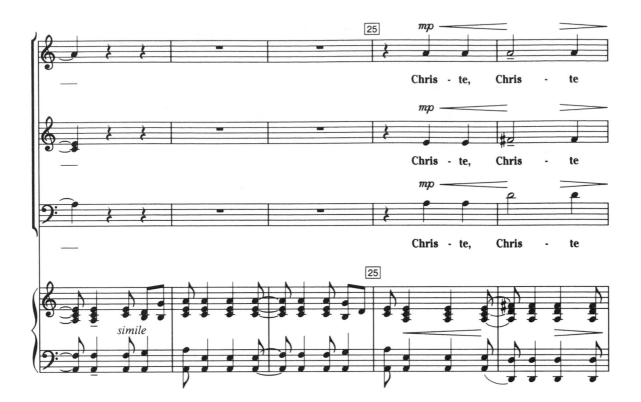

le - i son   Chris -te e - le - i-son,   Chris -te e - le - i -

le - i - son,   e - le - i - son,   e - le - i -

le - i-son.   Chris -te e - le - i - son,   e - le - i -

son, e - le - i - son.

son, ___ e - le - i - son.

son, e - le - i - son.

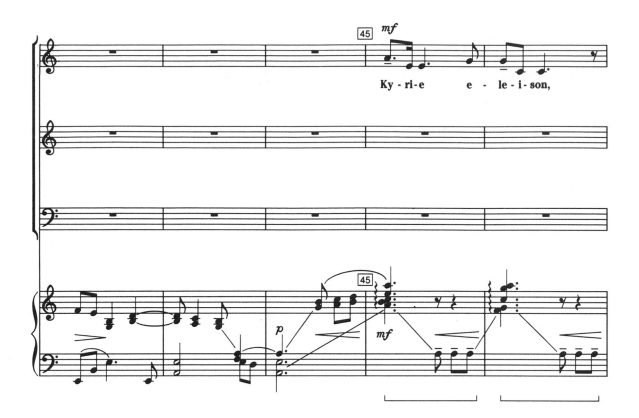

Lakota Wiyanki

Composer: Judith Herrington and Gail Woodside
Text: Traditional Lakota
Voicing: SATB

Focus

- Sing with proper vowel sounds.
- Perform music that represents the Native American culture.

SPOTLIGHT

To learn more about vowels, see page 55.

Getting Started

Even though you will find shopping malls, football stadiums and fast-food restaurants across our country, the United States is still rich with cultural diversity. Many American families preserve their heritage through traditional food, customs and music. List some of your family traditions. What other cultures are represented in your school or community? Our cultural background helps define who we are.

◆ History and Culture

"Lakota Wiyanki" is a Native American song in the Native American tradition. For the Lakota people, a song that has been "caught" belongs to the person who created it. Permission from the composer must be given before anyone else can use it. "Lakota Wiyanki," with its original Lakota words and melody, was caught by Cara Willowbrook. She then gave the song to her musician friend Gail Woodside, of the Apache Nation ancestry. When Gail received this gift, she in turn gave it to her friend Judith Herrington, who arranged and published the song for others to sing and enjoy.

The Lakota people (Teton dialect) are part of the Sioux Nation. Also included in the Sioux Nation are the Dakota people (Santee dialect) and the Nakota people (Yankton dialect). The English translation of the Lakota texts says, "Beautiful woman, standing with courage—with pride, you will go forward."

Links to Learning

◆ Vocal

Perform the following example to focus on vowel placement. Keep the "ay," "ah" and "oh" vowels forward with your jaw dropped to an open, relaxed position. The **fermata** (𝄐) is *a symbol that indicates to hold a note longer than its given value.*

Hay,— yah,— yoh.   Hay,— yah,— yoh.   Hay,— yah,— yoh. (etc.)

◆ Theory

Read and perform the following examples to establish an accent on the first beat of each measure when changing from $\frac{3}{4}$ meter to $\frac{4}{4}$ meter. **Meter** is *the organization of rhythm in music.*

◆ Artistic Expression

To learn more about the Lakota and other Native American cultures, divide into groups and research Native American poets and poetry. Choose your favorite poem and read it to the class.

Evaluation

Demonstrate how well you have learned the skills and concepts featured in the lesson "Lakota Wiyanki" by completing the following:

- In a **quartet** (*four singers*) with two on a part, perform measures 6–16, demonstrating the use of proper vowel sounds. Tenors, sing the part that best fits your voice. Rate your use of proper vowel sounds on a scale of 1 to 5, with 5 being the best.

- Organize a performance of "Lakota Wiyanki" that includes the Native American poetry found by your classmates. What did you learn from the poems? In what ways can the reading and studying of these Native American poems enhance your performance of "Lakota Wiyanki"?

Lakota Wiyanki

For SATB, a cappella with Optional Percussion

Arranged by
**JUDITH HERRINGTON
and GAIL WOODSIDE**

Traditional

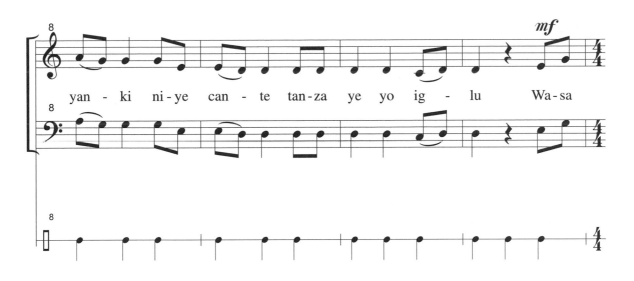

yan - ki ni - ye can - te tan - za ye yo ig - lu Wa - sa

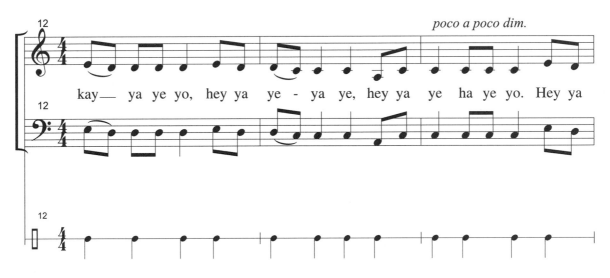

kay— ya ye yo, hey ya ye - ya ye, hey ya ye ha ye yo. Hey ya

ye— ya ye, hey ya ye ha ye yo. La -

La - ko - ta

(slide hands, rubbing palms, fingertips pointed forward)

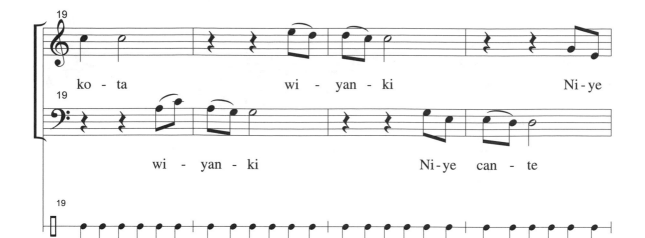

ko - ta   wi - yan - ki   Ni - ye

wi - yan - ki   Ni - ye   can - te

can - te   tan - za ye yo   tan - za ye   yo,   tan - za

tan - za ye yo   ig - lu,   ig - lu.

tacet sliding hands   *frame drum*

soprano

ye yo_____   Hey   ya hey - ya   hey__ yo__

alto

La - ko - ta wi - yan - ki   Ni - ye can - te   tan - za

tenor/bass

La - ko - ta wi - yan - ki   Ni - ye can - te   tan - za

Miserere Nobis

Composer: Victor Johnson
Text: Traditional Latin
Voicing: 3-Part Mixed

VOCABULARY
mass
intonation

SPOTLIGHT

To learn more about careers in music,
see page 128.

Focus

• Sing with pure Latin vowels.

• Perform music with understanding of the Latin text.

Getting Started

Composer Victor Johnson (b. 1978) graduated from the Booker T. Washington High School of Performing and Visual Arts in Dallas, Texas. He currently directs the Children's Choir of Texas at the Fort Worth Academy of Fine Arts. At the suggestion of his piano teacher, he began composing when he was in junior high. By the tenth grade, Johnson had his first piece of choral music published. He dedicated "Miserere Nobis" to the memory of his beloved piano teacher, Mrs. Carolyn Jones Campbell. Johnson knew at an early age, thanks to the encouragement of his piano teacher, that he wanted to pursue a career in music.

◆ History and Culture

The lyrics of "Miserere Nobis" are taken from the mass. The **mass** is *a religious service of prayers and ceremonies* that is commonly sung in Latin. The mass has many sections, some spoken and some sung. Composers traditionally set five of the sung sections to music, including the Kyrie, Gloria, Credo, Sanctus and Agnus Dei. German composer Johann Sebastian Bach's (1685–1750) *Mass in B Minor* is an example of this. A composer may also elect to set one section to music, as in American composer Samuel Barber's (1910–1981) *Agnus Dei.* Alternatively, as Victor Johnson has done, a composer may use some of the lyrics from a section. "Miserere Nobis" is from the Gloria.

Links to Learning

◆ Vocal

Latin is a lovely language to sing, in part because the vowels are pure. Read and perform the following example to practice singing the opening phrase and its repetitions with pure vowel sounds.

Mi - se - re - re,   mi - se - re - re,   mi - se - re - re   no - bis.

◆ Theory

The example below contains chords from measures 29–32. Perform the example below to practice singing choral patterns with good **intonation** (*the art of in-tune singing*).

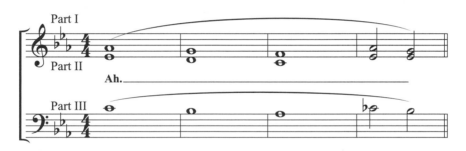

Ah.

◆ Artistic Expression

To develop artistry through singing in a foreign language, memorize the phrase-by-phrase translation of the Latin text given below.

Miserere nobis.	Have mercy on us.
Qui tollis peccata mundi,	Who takes away the sins of the world,
Suscipe deprecationem nostram.	Receive our prayer.
Quoniam tu solus sanctus,	You only are holy,
Tu solus Dominus,	You only are Lord, You only are most high.
Tu solus altissimus.	

Evaluation

Demonstrate how well you have learned the skills and concepts featured in the lesson "Miserere Nobis" by completing the following:

- Sing your part in measures 8–12 of "Miserere Nobis" using pure Latin vowels. Evaluate how well you did.

- With a partner, take turns reciting the Latin text while the other provides the English translation. Check each other's Latin pronunciation.

Miserere Nobis

For 3-Part Mixed and Piano

Traditional Latin

Words and Music by
VICTOR JOHNSON

re - re, mi-se - re - re no - bis.

re - re, mi-se - re - re no - bis.

re - re, mi-se - re no - bis.

Mi-se-re-re no-bis!

Mi-se-re-re no-bis!

Mi-se-re-re no-bis!

SPOTLIGHT

Musical Theater

There are many ways to tell a story. You may share a story with others through storytelling, acting, drawing and even singing. When you add music and drama to the telling of a story, the storytelling becomes musical theater. **Musical theater** is *an art form that combines acting, singing and dancing to tell a story.* It also often includes staging, costumes, lighting and scenery.

The Broadway musical is an American invention. In reaction to the dramatic and often "stuffy" operas of the time, Americans invented their own version of musical theater that was less grandiose and spoke directly to the people. As New York City became a center of the arts and music, many musical theaters appeared on a street named Broadway. As a result, the word *Broadway* came to be identified with stage and music productions.

Broadway musicals blossomed during the 1920s and 1930s with the works of George Gershwin, Cole Porter and Irving Berlin. By the 1950s, the Broadway musical was well established. The composer/lyricist team of Frederick Lowe and Alan Jay Lerner wrote *My Fair Lady* (1956) and *Camelot* (1961). Some of the masterpieces created by the team of Richard Rogers and Oscar Hammerstein II include *Oklahoma!* (1943), *Carousel* (1945) and *The Sound of Music* (1959). More recently, the composers Andrew Lloyd Webber and Stephen Sondheim have contributed to the continued success of Broadway musicals. Lloyd Webber's *Cats* (1981) and *The Phantom of the Opera* (1988) are two of the longest-running musicals in Broadway history.

Many are involved in the production of a Broadway musical, but it is the performers who bring the story to life through their singing, dancing and acting. If you have seen a musical or performed in one, you know how exciting it can be. For many, musical theater is indeed storytelling at its best!

The River Sleeps Beneath The Sky

Composer: Mary Lynn Lightfoot
Text: Paul Laurence Dunbar
Voicing: 3-Part Mixed

VOCABULARY

legato

word stress

dot

imitation

 SKILL BUILDERS

To learn more about dotted rhythms, see Intermediate Sight-Singing, *pages 45 and 89.*

Focus

- Demonstrate musical artistry.
- Read and perform dotted rhythms.
- Relate music to poetry.

Getting Started

Have you ever heard someone say, "I'd give anything for a little peace and quiet"? In our noisy world, it is difficult to stop and find a quiet place. In addition to spending time talking to others, we must also spend time communicating with ourselves. A place so peaceful and quiet is beautifully described in "The River Sleeps Beneath The Sky." As you sing, let the **legato** (*a connected and sustained style of singing*), musical lines and the intriguing poetry take you to a peaceful sunset at the end of a day.

◆ History and Culture

Paul Laurence Dunbar (1872–1906) was the first African American poet to attain international acclaim. He wrote short stories, poems and a novel. Dunbar grew up in Dayton, Ohio. He wanted to study law, but his family was too poor to pay for his education. Poverty, however, could not suppress his love of life and the ability to express it in prose and poetry. Dunbar died from tuberculosis at the age of thirty-three. The following poem, written by Dunbar, is inscribed on the Dayton Public Library:

> *Because I have loved so deeply*
> *Because I have loved so long,*
> *God in His great compassion*
> *Gave me the gift of song.*

Links to Learning

◆ Vocal

To sing expressively, it is important to create a rise and fall to the phrase by using proper word stress. Expressive **word stress** occurs when *important parts of the text are sung in a more accented style.* Perform the following example to develop expressive phrasing and word stress.

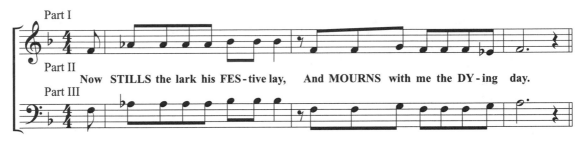

◆ Theory

Perform the following examples to develop skill in reading dotted rhythmic patterns in $\frac{4}{4}$ time. A **dot** is *a symbol that is placed to the right of a given note to increase the length of the note by half its value.*

◆ Artistic Expression

To develop artistry through expressive singing, form two groups of three to five singers. Practice performing the vocal imitation found in measures 11–14 of the song. In these measures **imitation,** or *the successive statement of a melody, theme or motive by two or more parts,* occurs both in the text and music. Follow the dynamic markings and make the music fade, just as the sun is fading away.

Evaluation

Demonstrate how well you have learned the skills and concepts featured in the lesson "The River Sleeps Beneath The Sky" by completing the following:

- Sing your part from measures 32–35, demonstrating your ability to sing in a legato style using expressive word stress. How could you sing more expressively?

- Perform the rhythmic patterns found in the Theory section above. Then, create your own dotted rhythmic pattern in $\frac{4}{4}$ meter. Check your work for rhythmic accuracy and correct notation.

For the choirs of Frontier Trail Junior High School, Olathe, Kansas, Sherri Porterfield, Director

The River Sleeps Beneath The Sky

For 3-Part Mixed and Piano

Words from "Sunset" by
PAUL LAURENCE DUNBAR (1872–1906)

Music by
MARY LYNN LIGHTFOOT

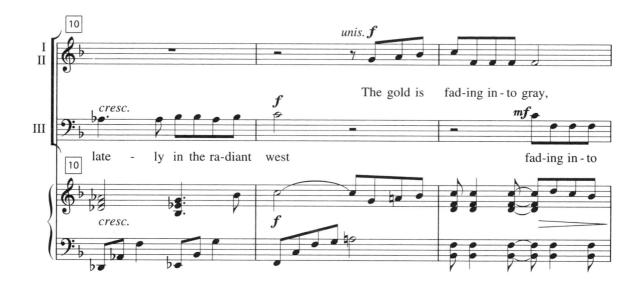

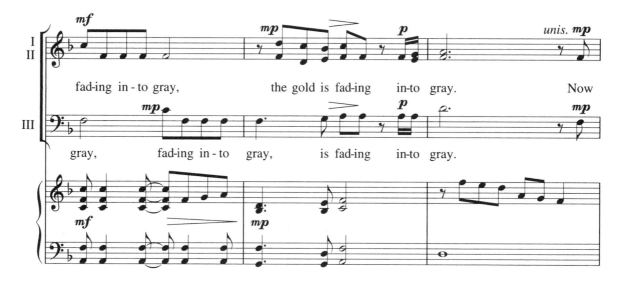

space.

space.

poco rit.

32 **Tempo I**
mp unis.

The riv-er sleeps be - neath the sky,

poco rit.

mp

32 **Tempo I**

poco rit. *mp*

And holds the shad-ows to its breast; The cres-cent moon___ shines

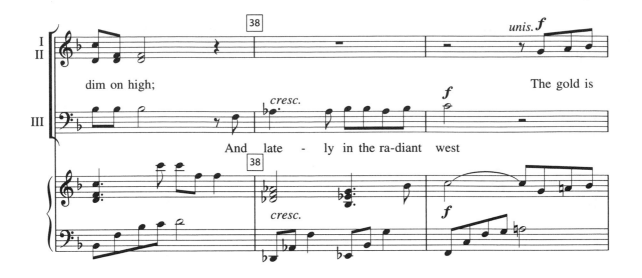

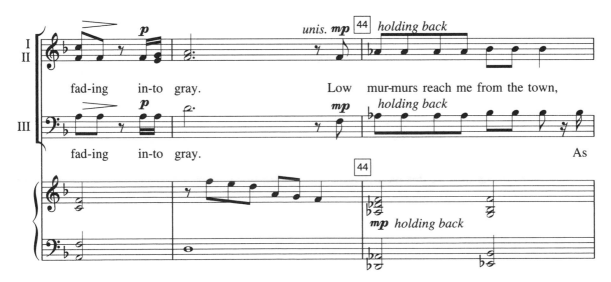

And shakes her man-tle dark-ly down.

Day puts on her som-bre crown,

a tempo

Sun - set, sun - set, sun - set,

The riv-er sleeps _____ be-neath the sky. Oh, it is

Sun - set, _____

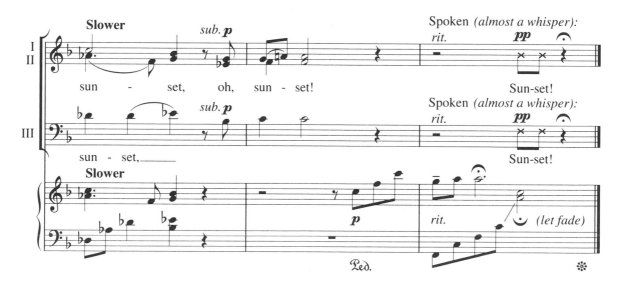

sun - set, oh, sun - set! Sun-set!

sun - set, _____ Sun-set!

Set Me As A Seal

Composer: John Leavitt
Text: Song of Solomon 8:6–7
Voicing: SATB

VOCABULARY

staggered entrances

homophony

D.C. al Fine

$\frac{4}{4}$ meter

breath support

Focus

- Identify compositional techniques found in the music.
- Read and write music in $\frac{4}{4}$ meter.
- Demonstrate musical artistry through the use of proper breath management.

Getting Started

"Set Me As A Seal" is a song about commitment. What is commitment? It is a promise you make to someone that you will hold up your end of the bargain. If you join a soccer, baseball or football team, you have a commitment to attend practices and the games. When you join a choir, you have a commitment to do your best and to attend rehearsals and performances. "Set Me As A Seal" describes the commitment of love.

SPOTLIGHT

To learn more about breath management, page 83.

◆ History and Culture

Several musical writing techniques are found in "Set Me As A Seal." The song begins with **staggered entrances** (*a technique in which the voices enter at different times*). The Altos enter first, followed by the Basses, Tenors and, finally, the Sopranos. At measure nine, **homophony,** or *music that consists of two or more voice parts with similar or identical rhythms*, is found. Then, at the very end you will find a **D.C. al Fine**. D.C. ("da capo") is *a term that indicates to go back to the beginning and repeat. The term* al fine *is a term that indicates to sing to the end or "fine."*

The text to "Set Me As A Seal" describes the "seal" as an official commitment of love. The seal upon the heart represents love, whereas the seal upon the arm represents protection and strength. What other descriptors of love can you find in this text?

Links to Learning

◆ Vocal

The character of this piece indicates a need for warmth of choral tone. Read and perform the following example to practice singing with uniform vowel sounds to enhance the richness of tone.

◆ Theory

Perform the example below to practice reading rhythmic patterns in $\frac{4}{4}$ **meter** (*a time signature in which there are four beats per measure and the quarter note receives the beat*). Conduct the pattern as you read.

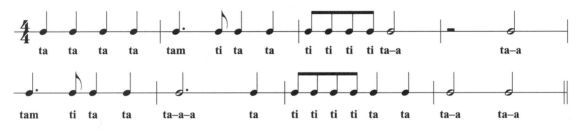

◆ Artistic Expression

"Set Me As A Seal" is written with a flowing melodic line. **Breath support** (*the constant airflow necessary to produce sound for singing*) is required to sing through the phrases without taking a breath. Sing measures 8–12 in one breath. Place your index finger to your lips as you begin to sing. Slowly move the finger away from your mouth in a slow, continuous motion. Think of the breath reaching out to your finger as you sing through the phrase.

Evaluation

Demonstrate how well you have learned the skills and concepts featured in the lesson "Set Me As A Seal" by completing the following:

- Define and locate in the music the following compositional techniques: staggered entrances, homophony and D.C. al Fine. Compare your answers with those of a classmate.

- Compose a four-measure rhythmic phrase in $\frac{4}{4}$ meter. Use the music as a guide. Check your work for rhythmic accuracy.

Set Me As A Seal

For SATB, a cappella

Text from Song of Solomon 8:6–7

Music by JOHN LEAVITT

Sing Out This Maytime

Composer: Johann Hermann Schein (1586–1630), edited by Patrick M. Liebergen
Text: Johann Hermann Schein, English text by Patrick M. Liebergen
Voicing: SAB

VOCABULARY

form

ABA form

articulation

$\frac{3}{4}$ meter

dynamics

 SKILL BUILDERS

To learn more about $\frac{3}{4}$ meter, see Intermediate Sight-Singing, *page 17.*

Focus

- Identify music forms found in music (ABA).
- Perform independently with accurate rhythm.
- Perform music with varying dynamics.

Getting Started

What are some of your favorite springtime activities? Maybe you enjoy playing ball, biking or in-line skating. And if you live in a place where winters are particularly cold, then as the weather warms up you might enjoy putting away your heavy coat and boots. The words of "Sing Out This Maytime" mention events that signal the beginning of spring, such as flowers blooming and nightingales singing.

◆ History and Culture

Johann Hermann Schein (1586–1630) was one of three leading German composers of his generation. When he was thirteen, Schein was a Soprano in his country's best choir, which was sponsored by the Elector of Saxony in Dresden. As an adult, Schein was appointed Thomascantor in Leipzig, Germany. One hundred years later, Johann Sebastian Bach, the most famous of German Baroque composers, worked at the same church.

Form is *the structure or design of a musical composition.* "Sing Out This Maytime" is written in ABA form. **ABA form** is *the design in which the opening phrases (section A) are followed by contrasting phrases (section B), which lead to a repetition of the opening phrases (Section A).* Locate these sections in the music.

Links to Learning

◆ Vocal

Perform the following example to practice correct articulation of quarter notes. **Articulation** is *the amount of separation or connection between notes.* In "Sing Out This Maytime," the quarter notes need to be distinct, yet also connected to the next pitch. To achieve this articulation, it is useful to imagine pressing into each tone gently, as if pressing your thumb into a sponge.

Dah, dah, dah, dah, dah, dah, dah, dah, dah.

◆ Theory

$\frac{3}{4}$ **meter** is *a time signature in which there are three beats per measure and the quarter note receives the beat.* Sometimes at a fast tempo, $\frac{3}{4}$ meter is conducted with one beat per measure. Read and perform the example below to practice reading rhythmic patterns in three. Begin at a slow tempo. When accurate, increase the tempo gradually until you feel only one beat in each measure.

ta ta ta   ta–a   ta   ta–a   ta   ta–a–a   ta   ti ti ta   tam   ti ta   ta ta–a   ta–a–a

◆ Artistic Expression

To develop artistry through expressive singing, follow the dynamic marks placed in the music by the editor. **Dynamics** are *symbols used in music to indicate how loud or soft to sing a passage.* The markings in this song include *mf* (medium loud), *mp* (medium soft) and *f* (loud). Be attentive to sing the repetition of each phrase softly.

Evaluation

Demonstrate how well you have learned the skills and concepts featured in the lesson "Sing Out This Maytime" by completing the following:

- Describe the form of "Sing Out This Maytime." Identify the measure number that marks the beginning of each section (ABA).

- Sing measures 59–70 to show your understanding of $\frac{3}{4}$ meter. How did you do?

- Perform measures 29–56 to show your ability to sing the repeated phrases in this song with accurate dynamics. How well are you able to demonstrate varied dynamics while singing?

Sing Out This Maytime
(Der kühle Maien)

For SAB and Piano with Optional Flutes*

Edited with English Text by
PATRICK M. LIEBERGEN

JOHANN HERMANN SCHEIN
(1586–1630)

* **Flute parts may be found on pages 225 and 226**

bloom   is   found;   A   shep - herd's joy - ful
Schä - fe - lein   mit   sei - nen Blü - me -

sound   is   heard_____   all   a - round!
lein   jetz - und_____   er - freu - en!

9

13

17
mp

Sing   out   this   May - time!   In   Spring   the
Der   küh - le   Mai - en   tut   Hirt   und

mp

mp

17

bloom is found; A shep - herd's joy - ful
Schä - fe - lein mit sei - nen Blü - me -

sound is heard_____ all a - round.
lein jetzt - und_____ er - freu - en.

The night - in - gale with cheer - ful
Frau Nach - ti - gall lässt ih - ren

song   re - joic - es   for   Spring   is

Schall   *im*   *grü - nen Wald*   *an - hö -*

here;   Ev - 'ry - one   sing,

ren;   *All*   *Vö - ge - lein*

let   your   voice   ring   with   mu - sic   re -

mit   *stim - men*   *ein,*   *die*   *Wald - mu - sik*

let your voice ring with mu - sic re - sound - ing
mit stim - men ein, die Wald - mu - sik ver - meh -

clear! Sing out this
ren. Der küh - le

May - time! In Spring the bloom is
Mai - en tut Hirt und Schä - fe -

found;   A   shep - herd's joy - ful sound is
lein   *mit*   *sei - nen Blü - me - lein jetzt-*

heard_____ all a - round!
und_____ er - freu - en!

Sing Out This Maytime

(Der kühle Maien)

FLUTE I

JOHANN HERMANN SCHEIN (1586–1630)
Edited by PATRICK M. LIEBERGEN

Sing Out This Maytime
(Der kühle Maien)

FLUTE II

JOHANN HERMANN SCHEIN (1586–1630)
Edited by PATRICK M. LIEBERGEN

The Wells Fargo Wagon

Composer: Meredith Willson, arranged by Roger Emerson
Text: Meredith Willson
Voicing: SAB

VOCABULARY

diction

syncopation

Focus

- Demonstrate musical artistry through the use of proper diction.
- Read and perform syncopated rhythmic patterns.
- Perform music that represents the musical theater genre.

SPOTLIGHT

To learn more about musical theater, see page 203.

Getting Started

Have you ever waited eagerly for the mailman to arrive? Perhaps you were expecting a special card, letter or package. Although we now enjoy daily mail delivery, in the 1800s some places in America might have received mail only once a month. As people moved further west, the delivery wagons would bring not only the mail, but also the many items ordered from catalogs. The song "The Wells Fargo Wagon" describes the great excitement and anticipation of the delivery wagon coming through the area.

◆ History and Culture

Wells Fargo and Company was founded in 1852 by Henry Wells and William G. Fargo. It provided express and banking between the East and California. At that time, it took fifteen days to travel by stagecoach from Nebraska to California!

"The Wells Fargo Wagon" is from the Broadway musical *The Music Man*, written by Meredith Willson in 1957. The show tells the humorous story about Professor Harold Hill, a traveling salesman and smooth-talking con artist. Hill convinces the citizens of River City, Iowa, that he can teach their children to play in a marching band if they purchase his instruments. In addition to "The Wells Fargo Wagon," *The Music Man* also features the song "Seventy-Six Trombones," among others.

Links to Learning

◆ Vocal

Clear **diction** *(the way a singer pronounces the words while singing)* is needed to convey the many words found in "The Wells Fargo Wagon." Chant the words to the text from measures 19–29. Begin slowly and then gradually increase the tempo. Exaggerate the beginning and ending consonants of every word.

◆ Theory

Read and perform the following rhythmic patterns found in "The Wells Fargo Wagon." The rest at the beginning of the measure creates *a shift of the accent from the strong portion of the beat to the weak portion of the beat.* This is called **syncopation.**

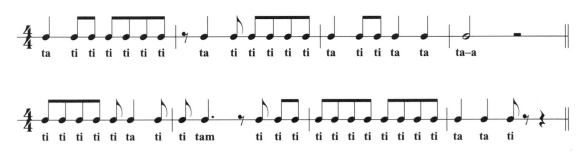

◆ Artistic Expression

Find and read a synopsis of *The Music Man.* List the characters and write a short description for each. Where in the story do they sing "The Wells Fargo Wagon"? Discuss the plot action before and after the song.

Evaluation

Demonstrate how well you have learned the skills and concepts featured in the lesson "The Wells Fargo Wagon" by completing the following:

- With a partner, chant the words of the song one section at a time. Coach each other until you are able to pronounce the words with clear diction.

- Clap the rhythms of the Theory section above to show your understanding of syncopation. Rate your ability to clap syncopated rhythms correctly based on a scale of 1 to 5, with 5 being the best.

From Meredith Willson's THE MUSIC MAN

The Wells Fargo Wagon

For SAB and Piano

Arranged by
ROGER EMERSON

Words and Music by
MEREDITH WILLSON

dare to make—— a stop, un - til you

dare to make—— a stop, un - til you

stop for me! _____

stop for me! _____

Glossary

CHORAL MUSIC TERMS

2/2 meter A time signature in which there are two beats per measure and the half note receives the beat.

2/4 meter A time signature in which there are two beats per measure and the quarter note receives the beat.

3/2 meter A time signature in which there are three beats per measure and the half note receives the beat.

3/4 meter A time signature in which there are three beats per measure and the quarter note receives the beat.

3/8 meter A time signature in which there is one group of three eighth notes per measure and the dotted quarter note receives the beat. When the tempo is very slow, this meter can be counted as having three beats per measure, with the eighth note receiving the beat.

4/4 meter A time signature in which there are four beats per measure and the quarter note receives the beat.

5/8 meter A time signature in which there are five beats per measure and the eighth note receives the beat.

6/4 meter A time signature in which there are two groups of three quarter notes per measure and the dotted half note receives the beat. When the tempo is very slow, this meter can be counted as having six beats per measure, with the quarter note receiving the beat.

6/8 meter A time signature in which there are two groups of three eighth notes per measure and the dotted quarter note receives the beat. When the tempo is very slow, this meter can be counted as having six beats per measure, with the eighth note receiving the beat.

9/8 meter A time signature in which there are three groups of three eighth notes per measure and the dotted quarter note receives the beat. When the tempo is very slow, this meter can be counted as having nine beats per measure, with the eighth note receiving the beat.

12/8 meter A time signature in which there are four groups of three eighth notes per measure and the dotted quarter note receives the beat.

A

a cappella *(ah-kah-PEH-lah)* [It.] A style of singing without instrumental accompaniment.

a tempo *(ah TEM-poh)* [It.] A tempo marking which indicates to return to the original tempo of a piece or section of music.

ABA form A form in which an opening section (A) is followed by a contrasting section (B), which leads to the repetition of the opening section (A).

accelerando *(accel.)* *(ah-chel-leh-RAHN-doh)* [It.] A tempo marking that indicates to gradually get faster.

accent A symbol placed above or below a given note to indicate that the note should receive extra emphasis or stress. ( )

accidental Any sharp, flat or natural that is not included in the key signature of a piece of music.

adagio *(ah-DAH-jee-oh)* [It.] Slow tempo, but not as slow as *largo*.

ad libitum *(ad. lib.)* [Lt.] An indication that the performer may vary the tempo or add or delete a vocal or instrumental part.

Aeolian scale *(ay-OH-lee-an)* [Gk.] A modal scale that starts and ends on *la*. It is made up of the same arrangement of whole and half steps as a natural minor scale.

al fine *(ahl FEE-neh)* [It.] To the end.

aleatory music *(AY-lee-uh-toh-ree)* A type of music in which certain aspects are performed randomly. Also known as chance music.

alla breve Indicates cut time; a duple meter in which there are two beats per measure, and half note receives the beat. *See* cut time.

allargando (*allarg.*) (*ahl-ahr-GAHN-doh*) [It.] To broaden, become slower.

allegro (*ah-LEH-groh*) [It.] Brisk tempo; faster than *moderato*, slower than *vivace*.

allegro non troppo (*ah-LEH-groh nohn TROH-poh*) [It.] A tempo marking that indicates not too fast. Not as fast as *allegro*.

altered pitch Another name for an accidental.

alto (*AL-toh*) The lowest-sounding female voice.

andante (*ahn-DAHN- teh*) [It.] Moderately slow; a walking tempo.

andante con moto (*ahn-DAHN- teh kohn MOH-toh*) [It.] A slightly faster tempo, "with motion."

animato Quickly, lively; "animated."

anthem A choral composition in English using a sacred text.

arpeggio (*ahr-PEH-jee-oh*) [It.] A chord in which the pitches are sounded successively, usually from lowest to highest; in broken style.

arrangement A piece of music in which a composer takes an existing melody and adds extra features or changes the melody in some way.

arranger A composer who takes an original or existing melody and adds extra features or changes the melody in some way.

art song A musical setting of a poem.

articulation The amount of separation or connection between notes.

articulators The lips, teeth, tongue and other parts of the mouth and throat that are used to produce vocal sound.

avocational Not related to a job or career.

B

barbershop A style of *a cappella* singing in which three parts harmonize with the melody. The lead sings the melody while the tenor harmonizes above and the baritone and bass harmonize below.

barcarole A Venetian boat song.

baritone The male voice between tenor and bass.

barline A vertical line placed on the musical staff that groups notes and rests together.

Baroque period (*bah-ROHK*) [Fr.] The historical period in Western civilization from 1600 to 1750.

bass The lowest-sounding male voice.

bass clef A clef that generally indicates notes that sound lower than middle C.

basso continuo (*BAH-soh cun-TIN-you-oh*) [It.] A continually moving bass line, common in music from the Baroque period.

beat The steady pulse of music.

bebop style Popular in jazz, music that features notes that are light, lively and played quickly. Often the melodic lines are complex and follow unpredictable patterns.

blues scale An altered major scale that uses flatted or lowered third, fifth and seventh notes: *ma* (lowered from *mi*), *se* (lowered from *sol*) and *te* (lowered from *ti*).

blues style An original African American art form that developed in the early twentieth century in the Mississippi Delta region of the South. The lyrics often express feelings of frustration, hardship or longing. It often contains elements such as call and response, the blues scale and swing.

body percussion The use of one's body to make a percussive sound, such as clapping, snapping or stepping.

breath mark A symbol in vocal music used to indicate where a singer should take a breath. (⸴)

breath support A constant airflow necessary to produce sound for singing.

cadence A melodic or harmonic structure that marks the end of a phrase or the completion of a song.

call and response A derivative of the field hollers used by slaves as they worked. A leader or group sings a phrase (call) followed by a response of the same phrase by another group.

calypso A style of music that originated in the West Indies and which features syncopated rhythms and comical lyrics.

canon A musical form in which one part sings a melody, and the other parts sing the same melody, but enter at different times. Canons are sometimes called rounds.

cantabile *(con-TAH-bee-leh)* [It.] In a lyrical, singing style.

cantata *(con-TAH-tah)* [It.] A large-scale musical piece made up of several movements for singers and instrumentalists. Johann Sebastian Bach was a prominent composer of cantatas.

cantor *(CAN-tor)* A person who sings and/or teaches music in a temple or synagogue.

canzona [It.] A rhythmic instrumental composition that is light and fast-moving.

chamber music Music performed by a small instrumental ensemble, generally with one instrument per part. The string quartet is a popular form of chamber music, consisting of two violins, a viola and a cello. Chamber music was popular during the Classical period.

chantey *See* sea chantey.

chanteyman A soloist who improvised and led the singing of sea chanteys.

chest voice The lower part of the singer's vocal range.

chorale *(kuh-RAL)* [Gr.] Congregational song or hymn of the German Protestant Church.

chord The combination of three or more notes played or sung together at the same time.

chromatic scale *(kroh-MAT-tick)* [Gk.] A scale that consists of all half steps and uses all twelve pitches in an octave.

Classical period The historical period in Western civilization from 1750 to 1820.

clef The symbol at the beginning of a staff that indicates which lines and spaces represent which notes.

coda A special ending to a song. A concluding section of a composition. (⊕)

common time Another name for 4/4 meter. Also known as common meter. (**C**)

composer A person who takes a musical thought and writes it out in musical notation to share it with others.

compound meter Any meter in which the dotted quarter note receives the beat, and the division of the beat is based on three eighth notes. 6/8, 9/8 and 12/8 are examples of compound meter.

con moto *(kohn MOH-toh)* [It.] With motion.

concert etiquette A term used to describe what is appropriate behavior in formal or informal musical performances.

concerto *(cun-CHAIR-toh)* [Fr., It.] A composition for a solo instrument and orchestra.

concerto grosso *(cun-CHAIR-toh GROH-soh)* [Fr., It.] A multimovement Baroque piece for a group of soloists and an orchestra.

conductor A person who uses hand and arm gestures to interpret the expressive elements of music for singers and instrumentalists.

conductus A thirteenth-century song for two, three or four voices.

consonance Harmonies in chords or music that are pleasing to the ear.

Contemporary period The historical period from 1900 to the present.

countermelody A separate melodic line that supports and/or contrasts the melody of a piece of music.

counterpoint The combination of two or more melodic lines. The parts move independently while harmony is created. Johann Sebastian Bach is considered by many to be one of the greatest composers of contrapuntal music.

contrary motion A technique in which two melodic lines move in opposite directions.

crescendo (*creh-SHEN-doh*) [It.] A dynamic marking that indicates to gradually sing or play louder. ⟨

cut time Another name for 2/2 meter. (₵)

D

da capo (*D.C.*) (*dah KAH-poh*) [It.] Go back to the beginning and repeat; *see* dal segno **and** al fine.

dal segno (*D.S.*) (*dahl SAYN-yah*) [It.] Go back to the sign and repeat.

D. C. al Fine (*FEE-nay*) [It.] A term that indicates to go back to the beginning and repeat. The term *al fine* indicates to sing to the end, or *fine*.

decrescendo (*DAY-creh-shen-doh*) [It.] A dynamic marking that indicates to gradually sing or play softer. ⟩

descant A special part in a piece of music that is usually sung higher than the melody or other parts of the song.

diatonic scale (*die-uh-TAH-nick*) A scale that uses no altered pitches or accidentals. Both the major scale and the natural minor scale are examples of a diatonic scale.

diction The pronunciation of words while singing.

diminished chord A minor chord in which the top note is lowered one half step from *mi* to *me*.

diminuendo (*dim.*) (*duh-min-yoo-WEN-doh*) [It.] Gradually getting softer; *see* decrescendo.

diphthong A combination of two vowel sounds.

dissonance A combination of pitches or tones that clash.

dolce (*DOHL-chay*) [It.] Sweetly.

dominant chord A chord built on the fifth note of a scale. In a major scale, this chord uses the notes *sol, ti* and *re*, and it may be called the **V** ("five") chord, since it is based on the fifth note of the major scale, or *sol*. In a minor scale, this chord uses the notes *mi, sol* and *ti* (or *mi, si* and *ti*), and it may be called the **v** or **V** ("five") chord, since it is based on the fifth note of the minor scale, or *mi*.

Dorian scale (*DOOR-ee-an*) [Gk.] A modal scale that starts and ends on *re*.

dot A symbol that increases the length of a given note by half its value. It is placed to the right of the note.

dotted half note A note that represents three beats of sound when the quarter note receives the beat. ♩.

double barline A set of two barlines that indicate the end of a piece or section of music.

D. S. al coda (*dahl SAYN-yoh ahl KOH-dah*) [It.] Repeat from the symbol (𝄋) and skip to the coda when you see the sign. (𝄌)

duet A group of two singers or instrumentalists.

dynamics Symbols in music that indicate how loud or soft to sing or play.

E

eighth note A note that represents one half beat of sound when the quarter note receives the beat. Two eighth notes equal one beat of sound when the quarter note receives the beat. ♪ ♫

eighth rest A rest that represents one half beat of silence when the quarter note receives the beat. Two eighth rests equal one beat of silence when the quarter note receives the beat. ♪

expressive singing To sing with feeling.

falsetto [It.] The register in the male voice that extends far above the natural voice. The light upper range.

fermata (*fur-MAH-tah*) [It.] A symbol that indicates to hold a note or rest for longer than its given value. (⌒)

fine (*fee-NAY*) [It.] A term used to indicate the end of a piece of music.

flat A symbol that lowers the pitch of a given note by one half step.(♭)

folk music Music that passed down from generation to generation through oral tradition. Traditional music that reflects a place, event or a national feeling.

folk song A song passed down from generation to generation through oral tradition. A song that reflects a place, event or a national feeling.

form The structure or design of a musical composition.

forte (*FOR-tay*) [It.] A dynamic that indicates to sing or play loud. (*f*)

fortissimo (*for-TEE-see-moh*) [It.] A dynamic that indicates to sing or play very loud. (*ff*)

fugue (*FYOOG*) A musical form in which the same melody is performed by different instruments or voices entering at different times, thus adding layers of sound.

fusion Music that is developed by the act of combining various types and cultural influences of music into a new style.

gospel music Religious music that originated in the African American churches of the South. This music can be characterized by improvisation, syncopation and repetition.

grand staff A staff that is created when two staves are joined

together.

grandioso [It.] Stately, majestic.

grave (*GRAH-veh*) [It.] Slow, solemn.

grazioso (*grah-tsee-OH-soh*) [It.] Graceful.

Gregorian chant A single, unaccompanied melodic line sung by male voices. Featuring a sacred text and used in the church, this style of music was developed in the Medieval period.

half note A note that represents two beats of sound when the quarter note receives the beat.

half rest A rest that represents two beats of silence when the quarter note receives the beat.

half step The smallest distance (interval) between two notes on a keyboard; the chromatic scale is composed entirely of half steps.

harmonic minor scale A minor scale that uses a raised seventh note, *si* (raised from *sol*).

harmonics Small whistle-like tones, or overtones, that are sometimes produced over a sustained pitch.

harmony A musical sound that is formed when two or more different pitches are played or sung at the same time.

head voice The higher part of the singer's vocal range.

homophonic (*hah-muh-FAH-nik*) [Gk.] A texture where all parts sing similar rhythm in unison or harmony.

homophony (*haw-MAW-faw-nee*) [Gk.] A type of music in which there are two or more parts with similar or identical rhythms being sung or played at the same time. Also, music in which melodic interest is concentrated in one voice part and may have subordinate accompaniment.

hushed A style marking indicating a soft, whispered tone.

I

imitation The act of one part copying what another part has already played or sung.

improvisation The art of singing or playing music, making it up as you go, or composing and performing a melody at the same time.

International Phonetic Alphabet (IPA) A phonetic alphabet that provides a notational standard for all languages. Developed in Paris, France in 1886.

interval The distance between two notes.

intonation The accuracy of pitch, in-tune singing.

Ionian scale (*eye-OWN-ee-an*) [Gk.] A modal scale that starts and ends on *do*. It is made up of the same arrangement of whole and half steps as a major scale.

J

jazz An original American style of music that features swing rhythms, syncopation and improvisation.

jongleur [Fr.] An entertainer who traveled from town to town during medieval times, often telling stories and singing songs.

K

key Determined by a song's or scale's home tone, or keynote.

key signature A symbol or set of symbols that determines the key of a piece of music.

L

ledger lines Short lines that appear above, between treble and bass clefs, or below the bass clef, used to expand the notation.

legato (*leh-GAH-toh*) [It.] A connected and sustained style of singing and playing.

lento (*LEN-toh*) [It.] Slow; a little faster than *largo*, a little slower than *adagio*.

lied (*leet*) [Ger.] A song in the German language, generally with a secular text.

liturgical text A text that has been written for the purpose of worship in a church setting.

lute An early form of the guitar.

Lydian scale (*LIH-dee-an*) [Gk.] A modal scale that starts and ends on *fa*.

lyrics The words of a song.

M

madrigal A poem that has been set to music in the language of the composer. Featuring several imitative parts, it usually has a secular text and is generally sung *a cappella*.

maestoso (*mah-eh-STOH-soh*) [It.] Perform majestically.

major chord A chord that can be based on the *do, mi,* and *sol* of a major scale.

major scale A scale that has *do* as its home tone, or keynote. It is made up of a specific arrangement of whole steps and half steps in the following order: W + W + H + W + W + W + H.

major tonality A song that is based on a major scale with *do* as its keynote, or home tone.

mangulina A traditional dance from the Dominican Republic.

marcato (*mar-CAH-toh*) [It.] A stressed and accented style of singing and playing.

mass A religious service of prayers and ceremonies originating in the Roman Catholic Church consisting of spoken and sung sections. It consists of several sections divided into two groups: proper (text changes for every day) and ordinary (text stays the same in every mass). Between the years 1400 and 1600, the mass assumed its present form consisting of the Kyrie, Gloria, Credo, Sanctus and Agnus Dei. It may include chants, hymns and psalms as well. The mass also developed into large musical works for chorus, soloists and even orchestra.

measure The space between two barlines.

Medieval period The historical period in Western civilization also known as the Middle Ages (400–1430).

medley A collection of songs musically linked together.

melisma *(muh-LIZ-mah)* [Gk.] A group of notes sung to a single syllable or word.

melismatic singing *(muh-liz-MAT-ik)* [Gk.] A style of text setting in which one syllable is sung over many notes.

melodic contour The overall shape of the melody.

melodic minor scale A minor scale that uses raised sixth and seventh notes: *fi* (raised from *fa*) and *si* (raised from *sol*). Often, these notes are raised in ascending patterns, but not in descending patterns.

melody A logical succession of musical tones.

meter A way of organizing rhythm.

meter signature **See** time signature.

metronome marking A sign that appears over the top line of the staff at the beginning of a piece or section of music that indicates the tempo. It shows the kind of note that will receive the beat and the number of beats per minute as measured by a metronome.

mezzo forte *(MEH-tsoh FOR tay)* [It.] A dynamic that indicates to sing or play medium loud. (*mf*)

mezzo piano *(MEH-tsoh pee-AH-noh)* [It.] A dynamic that indicates to sing or play medium soft. (*mp*)

mezzo voce *(MEH-tsoh VOH-cheh)* [It.] With half voice; reduced volume and tone.

minor chord A chord that can be based on the *la, do,* and *mi* of a minor scale.

minor scale A scale that has *la* as its home tone, or keynote. It is made up of a specific arrangement of whole steps and half steps in the following order: W + H +W + W + H + W + W.

minor tonality A song that is based on a minor scale with *la* as its keynote, or home tone.

mixed meter A technique in which the time signature or meter changes frequently within a piece of music.

Mixolydian scale *(mix-oh-LIH-dee-an)* [Gr.] A modal scale that starts and ends on *sol*.

modal scale A scale based on a mode. Like major and minor scales, each modal scale is made up of a specific arrangement of whole steps and half steps, with the half steps occurring between *mi* and *fa*, and *ti* and *do*.

mode An early system of pitch organization that was used before major and minor scales and keys were developed.

modulation A change in the key or tonal center of a piece of music within the same song.

molto [It.] Very or much; for example, *molto rit.* means "much slower."

motet *(moh-teht)* Originating as a Medieval and Renaissance polyphonic song, this choral form of composition became an unaccompanied work, often in contrapuntal style. Also, a short, sacred choral piece with a Latin text that is used in religious services but is not a part of the regular mass.

motive A shortened expression, sometimes contained within a phrase.

music critic   A writer who gives an evaluation of a musical performance.

music notation   Any means of writing down music, including the use of notes, rests and symbols.

musical   A play or film whose action and dialogue are combined with singing and dancing.

musical theater   An art form that combines acting, singing, and dancing to tell a story. It often includes staging, costumes, lighting and scenery.

mysterioso   [It.] Perform in a mysterious or haunting way; to create a haunting mood.

N

narrative song   A song that tells a story.

national anthem   A patriotic song adopted by nations through tradition or decree.

nationalism   Patriotism; pride of country. This feeling influenced many Romantic composers such as Wagner, Tchaikovsky, Dvorák, Chopin and Brahms.

natural   A symbol that cancels a previous sharp or flat, or a sharp or flat in a key signature. (♮)

natural minor scale   A minor scale that uses no altered pitches or accidentals.

no breath mark   A direction not to take a breath at a specific place in the composition. (N.B.)

non troppo (*nahn TROH-poh*)   [It.] Not too much; for example, *allegro non troppo*, "not too fast."

notation   Written notes, symbols and directions used to represent music within a composition.

O

octave   An interval of two pitches that are eight notes apart on a staff.

ode   A poem written in honor of a special person or occasion. These poems were generally dedicated to a member of a royal family. In music, an ode usually includes several sections for choir, soloists and orchestra.

opera   A combination of singing, instrumental music, dancing and drama that tells a story.

optional divisi (*opt.div.*)   Indicating a split in the music into optional harmony, shown by a smaller cued note.

oral tradition   Music that is learned through rote or by ear and is interpreted by its performer(s).

oratorio (*or-uh-TOR-ee-oh*)   [It.] A dramatic work for solo voices, chorus and orchestra presented without theatrical action. Usually, oratorios are based on a literary or religious theme.

ostinato (*ahs-tuh-NAH-toh*)   [It.] A rhythmic or melodic passage that is repeated continuosly.

overture   A piece for orchestra that serves as an introduction to an opera or other dramatic work.

P

palate   The roof of the mouth; the hard palate is at the front, the soft palate is at the back.

parallel motion   A technique in which two or more melodic lines move in the same direction.

parallel sixths   A group of intervals that are a sixth apart and which move at the same time and in the same direction.

parallel thirds   A group of intervals that are a third apart and which move at the same time and in the same direction.

part-singing   Two or more parts singing an independent melodic line at the same time.

patsch   The act of slapping one's hands on one's thighs.

pentatonic scale   A five-tone scale using the pitches *do, re, mi, sol* and *la*.

perfect fifth   An interval of two pitches that are five notes apart on a staff.

perfect fourth   An interval of two pitches that are four notes apart on a staff.

phrase   A musical idea with a beginning and an end.

Phrygian scale (*FRIH-gee-an*) [Gk.] A modal scale that starts and ends on *mi*.

pianissimo (*pee-ah-NEE-see-moh*) [It.] A dynamic that indicates to sing or play very soft. (*pp*)

piano (*pee-AH-noh*) [It.] A dynamic that indicates to sing or play soft. (*p*)

pitch Sound, the result of vibration; the highness or lowness of a tone, determined by the number of vibrations per second.

pitch matching In a choral ensemble, the ability to sing the same notes as those around you.

piu (*pew*) [It.] More; for example, *piu forte* means "more loudly."

poco (*POH-koh*) [It.] Little; for example *poco dim.* means "a little softer."

poco a poco (*POH-koh ah POH-koh*) [It.] Little by little; for example, *poco a poco cresc.* means "little by little increase in volume."

polyphony (*pah-LIH-fun-nee*) [Gk.] Literally, "many sounding." A type of music in which there are two or more different melodic lines being sung or played at the same time. Polyphony was refined during the Renaissance, and this period is sometimes called "golden age of polyphony."

polyrhythms A technique in which several different rhythms are performed at the same time.

presto (*PREH-stoh*) [It.] Very fast.

program music A descriptive style of music composed to relate or illustrate a specific incident, situation or drama; the form of the piece is often dictated or influenced by the nonmusical program. This style commonly occurs in music composed during the Romantic period.

Q

quarter note A note that represents one beat of sound when the quarter note receives the beat.

quarter rest A rest that represents one beat of silence when the quarter note receives the beat.

quartet A group of four singers or instrumentalists.

R

rallentando (*rall.*) (*rahl-en-TAHN-doh*) [It.] Meaning to "perform more and more slowly." *See* ritard.

refrain A repeated section at the end of each phrase or verse in a song. Also known as a chorus.

register, vocal A term used for different parts of the singer's range, such as head register, or head voice (high notes); and chest register, or chest voice (low notes).

relative minor scale A minor scale that shares the same key signature as its corresponding major scale. Both scales share the same half steps, between *mi* and *fa*, and *ti* and *do*.

Renaissance period The historical period in Western civilization from 1430 to 1600.

repeat sign A symbol that indicates that a section of music should be repeated.

repetition The restatement of a musical idea; repeated pitches; repeated "A" section in ABA form.

requiem (*REK-wee-ehm*) [Lt.] Literally, "rest." A mass written and performed to honor the dead and comfort the living.

resonance Reinforcement and intensification of sound by vibration.

rest A symbol used in music notation to indicate silence.

rhythm The combination of long and short notes and rests in music. These may move with the beat, faster than the beat or slower than the beat.

ritard *(rit.) (ree-TAHRD)* [It.] A tempo marking that indicates to gradually get slower.

Romantic period The historical period in Western civilization from 1820 to 1900.

rondo form A form in which a repeated section is separated by several contrasting sections.

rote The act of learning a song by hearing it over and over again.

round *See* canon.

rubato *(roo-BAH-toh)* [It.] The freedom to slow down and/or speed up the tempo without changing the overall pulse of a piece of music.

S

sacred music Music associated with religious services or themes.

scale A group of pitches that are sung or played in succession and are based on a particular home tone, or keynote.

scat singing An improvisational style of singing that uses nonsense syllables instead of words. It was made popular by jazz trumpeter Louis Armstrong.

sea chantey A song sung by sailors, usually in rhythm with their work.

secular music Music not associated with religious services or themes.

sempre *(SEHM-preh)* [It.] Always, continually.

sempre accelerando *(sempre accel.) (SEHM-preh ahk-chel)* [It.] A term that indicates to gradually increase the tempo of a piece or section of music.

sequence A successive musical pattern that begins on a higher or lower pitch each time it is repeated.

serenata [It.] A large-scale musical work written in honor of a special occasion. Generally performed in the evening or outside, it is often based on a mythological theme.

sforzando *(sfohr-TSAHN-doh)* [It.] A sudden strong accent on a note or chord. *(sfz)*

sharp A symbol that raises the pitch of a given note one half step. (♯)

shekere An African shaker consisting of a hollow gourd surrounded by beads.

sight-sing Reading and singing music at first sight.

simile *(sim.) (SIM-ee-leh)* [It.] To continue the same way.

simple meter Any meter in which the quarter note receives the beat, and the division of the beat is based on two eighth notes. 2/4, 3/4 and 4/4 are examples of simple meter.

singing posture The way one sits or stands while singing.

sixteenth note A note that represents one quarter beat of sound when the quarter note receives the beat. Four sixteenth notes equal one beat of sound when the quarter note receives the beat.

sixteenth rest A rest that represents one quarter beat of silence when the quarter note receives the beat. Four sixteenth rests equal one beat of silence when the quarter note receives the beat.

skipwise motion The movement from a given note to another note that is two or more notes above or below it on the staff.

slur A curved line placed over or under a group of notes to indicate that they are to be performed without a break.

solfège syllables Pitch names using *do, re, mi, fa, sol, la, ti, do,* etc.

solo One person singing or playing an instrument alone.

sonata-allegro form A large ABA form consisting of three sections: exposition, development and recapitulation. This form was made popular during the Classical period.

soprano The highest-sounding female voice.

sostenuto (*SAHS-tuh-noot-oh*) [It.] The sustaining of a tone or the slackening of tempo.

sotto voce In a quiet, subdued manner; "under" the voice.

spirito (*SPEE-ree-toh*) [It.] Spirited; for example, *con spirito* ("with spirit").

spiritual Songs that were first sung by African American slaves, usually based on biblical themes or stories.

staccato (*stah-KAH-toh*) [It.] A short and detached style of singing or playing.

staff A series of five horizontal lines and four spaces on which notes are written. A staff is like a ladder. Notes placed higher on the staff sound higher than notes placed lower on the staff.

stage presence A performer's overall appearance on stage, including enthusiasm, facial expression and posture.

staggered breathing In ensemble singing, the practice of planning breaths so that no two singers take a breath at the same time, thus creating the overall effect of continuous singing.

staggered entrances A technique in which different parts and voices enter at different times.

stanza A section in a song in which the words change on each repeat. Also known as a verse.

stepwise motion The movement from a given note to another note that is directly above or below it on the staff.

strophe A verse or stanza in a song.

strophic A form in which the melody repeats while the words change from verse to verse.

style The particular character of a musical work; often indicated by words at the beginning of a composition, telling the performer the general manner in which the piece is to be performed.

subdominant chord A chord built on the fourth note of a scale. In a major scale, this chord uses the notes *fa, la* and *do,* and it may be called the **IV** ("four") chord, since it is based on the fourth note of the major scale, or *fa.* In a minor scale, this chord uses the notes *re, fa* and *la,* and it may be called the **iv** ("four") chord, since it is based on the fourth note of the minor scale, or *re.*

subito (sub.) (*SOO-bee-toh*) [It.] Suddenly.

suspension The holding over of one or more musical tones in a chord into the following chord, producing a momentary discord.

swing rhythms Rhythms in which the second eighth note of each beat is played or sung like the last third of triplet, creating an uneven, "swing" feel. A style often found in jazz and blues. Swing rhythms are usually indicated at the beginning of a song or section.

syllabic See syllabic singing.

syllabic singing A style of text setting in which one syllable is sung on each note.

syllabic stress The stressing of one syllable over another.

symphonic poem A single-movement work for orchestra, inspired by a painting, play or other literary or visual work. Franz Liszt was a prominent composer of symphonic poems. Also known as a tone poem.

symphony A large-scale work for orchestra.

syncopation The placement of accents on a weak beat or a weak portion of the beat, or on a note or notes that normally do not receive extra emphasis.

synthesizer A musical instrument that produces sounds electronically, rather than by the physical vibrations of an acoustic instrument.

tempo Terms in music that indicate how fast or slow to sing or play.

tempo I or tempo primo *See* a tempo.

tenor The highest-sounding male voice.

tenuto *(teh-NOO-toh)* [It.] A symbol placed above or below a given note indicating that the note should receive stress and/or that its value should be slightly extended. (♩)

text Words, usually set in a poetic style, that express a central thought, idea or narrative.

texture The thickness of the different layers of horizontal and vertical sounds.

theme A musical idea, usually a melody.

theme and variation form A musical form in which variations of the basic theme make up the composition.

third An interval of two pitches that are three notes apart on a staff.

tie A curved line used to connect two or more notes of the same pitch together in order to make one (♩ ♩) longer note.

tied notes Two or more notes of the same pitch connected together with a tie in order to make one longer note.

timbre The tone quality of a person's voice or musical instrument.

time signature The set of numbers at the beginning of a piece of music. The top number indicates the number of beats per measure. The bottom number indicates the kind of note that receives the beat. Time signature is sometimes called meter signature.

to coda Skip to (⊕) or CODA.

tone color That which distinguishes the voice or tone of one singer or instrument from another; for example, a soprano from an alto, or a flute from a clarinet. *See* timbre.

tonic chord A chord built on the home tone, or keynote of a scale. In a major scale, this chord uses the notes *do, mi* and *sol*, and it may be called the **I** ("one") chord, since it is based on the first note of the major scale, or *do*. In a minor scale, this chord uses the notes *la, do* and *mi*, and it may be called the **i** ("one") chord, since it is based on the first note of the minor scale, or *la*.

treble clef A clef that generally indicates notes that sound higher than middle C.

trio A group of three singers or instrumentalists with usually one on a part.

triplet A group of notes in which three notes of equal duration are sung in the time normally given to two notes of equal duration.

troppo *(TROHP-oh)* [It.] Too much; for example, *allegro non troppo* ("not too fast").

tutti *(TOO-tee)* [It.] Meaning "all" or "together."

twelve-tone music A type of music that uses all twelve tones of the scale equally. Developed in the early twentieth century, Arnold Schoenberg is considered to be the pioneer of this style of music.

two-part music A type of music in which two different parts are sung or played.

unison All parts singing or playing the same notes at the same time.

variation A modification of a musical idea, usually after its initial appearance in a piece.

vivace *(vee-VAH-chay)* [It.] Very fast; lively.

vocal jazz A popular style of music characterized by strong prominent meter, improvisation and dotted or syncopated patterns. Sometimes sung *a cappella.*

W

whole note   A note that represents four beats of sound when the quarter note receives the beat.   o

whole rest   A rest that represents four beats of silence when the quarter note receives the beat.   ▬

whole step   The combination of two successive half steps.

word painting   A technique in which the music reflects the meaning of the words.

word stress   The act of singing important parts of the text in a more accented style than the other parts.

Y

yoik   A vocal tradition of the Sámi people of the Arctic region of Sampi that features short melodic phrases that are repeated with slight variations.

Classified Index

A Cappella

Bless The Lord, O My Soul 92

Down In The Valley 10

Innsbruck, ich muss dich lassen 78

Lakota Wiyanki 186

Set Me As A Seal 212

Shalom Aleichem 56

Broadway

The Wells Fargo Wagon 227

Composers

Heinrich Isaac (c. 1450–1517)
Innsbruck, ich muss dich lassen 78

Johann Hermann Schein (1586–1630)
Sing Out This Maytime 216

George Frideric Handel (1685–1759)
Come Joyfully Sing 84

Johann Michael Haydn (1737–1806)
Rise Up This Day To Celebrate 2

Mikhail Ippolitov-Ivanov (1859–1935)
Bless The Lord, O My Soul 92

Noel Goemanne (b. 1927)
Sing To The Lord 100

Folk

African American Spiritual
Elijah Rock! 16

American
Bound For The Rio Grande 136
Down In The Valley 10

Irish
I Know Where I'm Goin' 168

Native American
Lakota Wiyanki 186

Foreign Language

Duoluo
Duond Akuru 156

German
Innsbruck, ich muss dich lassen 78
Sing Out This Maytime 216

Hebrew
Shalom Aleichem 56

Latin
Calypso Gloria 64
Kyrie 178
Miserere Nobis 194

Lakota
Lakota Wiyanki 186

Spanish
¡Aleluya, Amén! 130
Cantemos Alleluia 36

Gospel

City Called Heaven 148

Instruments

Bass
Calypso Gloria 64

Drums
¡Aleluya, Amén! 130

Flute
Duond Akuru 156
Sing Out This Maytime 216

Percussion
Calypso Gloria 64
Duond Akuru 156
Lakota Wiyanki 186

Trumpet
Rise Up This Day To Celebrate 2

Music & History

Renaissance
Innsbruck, ich muss dich lassen 78

Baroque
Come Joyfully Sing 84
Sing Out This Maytime 216

Classical
Rise Up This Day To Celebrate 2

Romantic
Bless The Lord, O My Soul 92

Contemporary
Sing To The Lord 100

Poetry

The River Sleeps Beneath The Sky . . 204

Seasonal, Patriotic

America The Beautiful 26
Calypso Gloria 64
Sing Out This Maytime 216
Winter Storm 46

Listening Selections

As Vesta Was Descending
 Thomas Weelkes 111

"Three Voltas" from *Terpsichore*
 Michael Praetorius 111

"Gloria in excelsis Deo"
 from *Gloria in D Major*
 Antonio Vivaldi 115

"The Arrival of the Queen of Sheba"
 from *Solomon*
 George Frideric Handel 115

"The Heavens Are Telling" from *Creation*
 Franz Joseph Haydn 119

Eine Kleine Nachtmusik, First Movement
 Wolfgang Amadeus Mozart 119

"Toreador Chorus" from *Carmen*
 Georges Bizet 123

The Moldau (excerpt)
 Bedrich Smetana 123

The Battle of Jericho
 arr. Moses Hogan 127

"Infernal Dance of King Kaschei"
 from *The Firebird*
 Igor Stravinsky 127

Index of Songs and Spotlights

¡Aleluya, Amén! 130
America The Beautiful 26
Bless The Lord, O My Soul 92
Bound For The Rio Grande 136
Calypso Gloria 64
Cantemos Alleluia 36
City Called Heaven 148
Come Joyfully Sing 84
Down In The Valley 10
Duond Akuru 156
Elijah Rock! 16
I Know Where I'm Goin' 168
Innsbruck, ich muss dich lassen 78
Kyrie 178
Lakota Wiyanki 186
Miserere Nobis 194
The River Sleeps Beneath The Sky 204
Rise Up This Day To Celebrate 2
Set Me As A Seal 212
Shalom Aleichem 56
Sing Out This Maytime 216
Sing To The Lord 100
The Wells Fargo Wagon 227
Winter Storm 46

Spotlights

Arranging 63
Breath Management 83
Careers In Music 128
Changing Voice 135
Concert Etiquette 99
Diction 25
Gospel Music 147
Improvisation 177
Musical Theater 203
Pitch Matching 77
Posture 35
Vowels 55

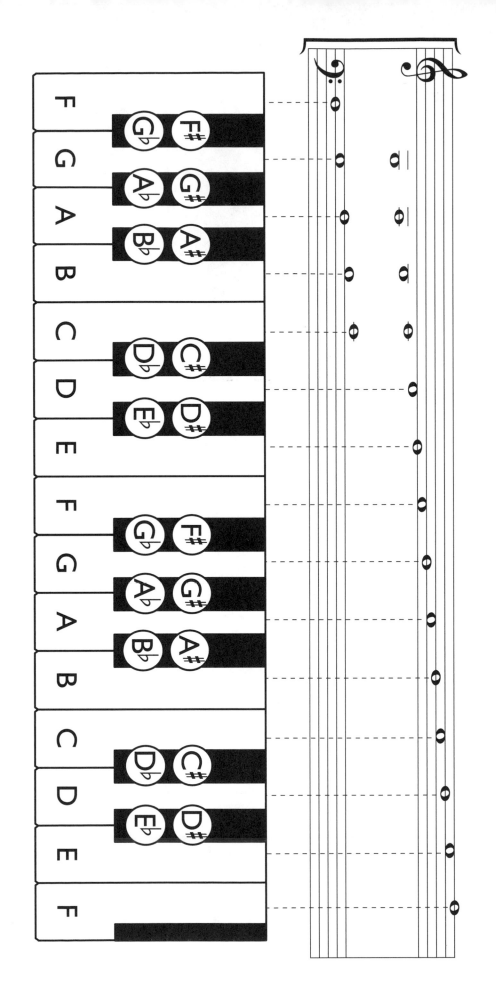